MARY ROBINSON

The Life and Times of an Irish Liberal

Michael O'Sullivan

BLACKWATER PRESS

419884

© 1993 Blackwater Press,
Broomhill Business Park,
Tallaght,
Dublin 24.

Produced in Ireland by Blackwater Press

ISBN 0 86121 448 X

To the memory of my grandmother, Elizabeth Parker Slattery

CONTENTS

Introduction

From time to time, and usually against considerable odds, an exceptional woman leaves an indelible mark on the public life of her country. In Ireland Mary Robinson is such a woman. This book is not about her remarkable achievement in transforming the office which she now holds from a near-dormant constitutional symbol into an active working presidency. The book's terminus is the point where she leaves St. Patrick's Hall at Dublin Castle, on Monday 3 December 1990, after her inauguration as the seventh President of Ireland.

As a constitutional lawyer, Mrs. Robinson was acutely aware of limitations of the office she had just entered upon. "There is a demarcation line," she said soon after her election, "I know where that demarcation line is, and I think the skill would be to use all of the space right up to the edge of that line." If there is a key statment in the Robinson canon, that is surely it.

Knowing where the demarcation line is drawn is the key to much of Mary Robinson's life and work. By any standards, both as lawyer and politician, she had an impressive career. For over 20 years she was one of the central characters in the most formative chapter in the history of Ireland's movement towards a pluralist society. That achievement has not been chronicled. If this book achieves anything, I hope it will be to redress that situation.

Her election as senator to the Dublin University (Trinity College) panel in 1969 was a watershed in the Senate representation of that ancient seat of Irish learning. As Mary T.W. Bourke she was not only the youngest woman ever elected senator in Ireland; she was also the first woman and the first Catholic to represent Trinity in the Upper House of the Irish Parliament. Her election to the Senate brought her to almost immediate national prominence.

Quite soon after her election, the question being asked in political circles was: who is this outspoken young senator? In the political watering holes, the question was sometimes put less politely. More significantly, the question being asked in numerous articles and interviews was: who is this woman? The aim of this book is to go some way towards answering that question.

Such is Mary Robinson's stature now that from the moment I announced

i

my intention to write this book I have been constantly questioned as to whether the book is authorised. The answer is no, it is not. At no time have I felt, however, that any blocks were put in the way of my research.

I have great pleasure in thanking the many people who helped me along the way.

I am greatly indebted to those members of the President's family who agreed to be interviewed, especially Mrs. Robinson's cousin, Mr. John Paget Bourke, who gave generously of his time and allowed me access to the photographic collection of his father, the late Sir Paget Bourke; also to Mrs. Robinson's brother, Mr. Adrian P. Bourke, for his memories of his sister and family.

In Ballina I owe much to Mr. P.J. Clarke, who made available his splendid collection of documents relating to the town's history and gave so generously of his time. Others in the town were also helpful, and they include Mr. Jackie Clarke, Mr. James McGuire and The Rev. Stanley Irvine. Mr. John Cooney and Mrs. Liguori Cooney gave generously of their time and hospitality.

Mr. Carey Harrison was, in many respects, midwife to the book and for his encouragement and generosity I am deeply indebted.

The book was read in manuscript by Mr. Edward Mulhall, Programme Editor (News) at RTE and also by Ms. Kathleen O'Meara of RTE News and formerly Press Officer of the Labour Party. I am very grateful to them for their many helpful suggestions.

Without the help of Mr. Eamon Ward I would not have been able to come to terms with the complexity of Mrs. Robinson's impressive legal career. I benefited greatly from his impeccable research and expert knowledge. In this regard I am also grateful to Mr. Kevin Costello of the Law Department of University College, Galway. Many friends and acquaintances in the Law Library have also helped with this section of the book.

Mr. Peter Slater and Mr. Ian O'Doherty gave invaluable help with the sections on Mrs. Robinson's Senate career and the presidential election. I am deeply indebted to them both. I am also grateful to Mr. Jerry Scanlan for his constant help and encouragement.

My task would have been a great deal more difficult were it not for the kind assistance given me by RTE's library staff, especially Ms. Jane Hall, Mr. Frank Kelly, Mr. Stephen D'arcy and Mr. Shay De Barra.

Mr. Tim Ryan of the *Irish Press* gave me access to the unpublished manuscript of his biography of the Labour leader Dick Spring.

The encouragement and assistance given to me by my friends Donal MacNally Jnr., and Deirdre Young, played no small part in the making of this book. I have very great pleasure in acknowledging that debt here.

Through the generosity of IBM Ireland, the computer technology on which this book was written was made available to me.

Anyone researching a book on Mary Robinson owes much to the splendid work done on the 1990 Presidential Election by Ms. Emily O'Reilly and Mr. Fergus Finlay, in their excellent books on the subject.

Others who provided material and assistance for the book include the Rt. Hon. Roy Bradford, Ms. Ruth Buchanan, Dr. Frank Callanan, Mr. Rory Carren, Mr. Peter Cluskey, Mrs. François Connelly, Ms. Adrienne Cullen, Mr. Val Dillon, Mr T.A. Dillon-Leetch, Mr. Billy Drake, Ms. Ann-Marie Franklin, Mr. John Gilmartin, Mr. Brendan Halligan, Mr. Reginald Hastings, Mr. Seamus Hosey, Prof. Brendan Kennelly, the late Mr. Patrick Lindsay, Mr. Edward Liston, Mr. Edmund Lynch, Mr. Rossa Lyons, Mr. Charles Edward Lysaght, Mr. Leslie Mallory, Mr. Tom Mathews, Mr. P.J. Mara, Ms. Mary Moreton, Ms. Christina Murphy, Mr. Desmond McAvock, Mr. Joseph McDonnell, Count Randal McDonnell, Ms. Dorothy McKane, Rev. Fr. Michael McKeon, Mr. Ian McMullan, Mr. Muiris Moynihan, Mr. Charles McGowan Mosley, Mr. Ciaran Nicholson, Mr. Anthony O Brien, Ms. Emily O'Reilly, Mr. Michael Ronayne, Ms. Patience Ryan, Ms. Fiona Scott, Ms. Lean Scully, Mr. Denis Staunton, Ms. Nell Stewart-Liberty, Mr. Diarmuid Teevan and Dr. W.E. Vaughan.

Several Libraries and Institutions were extremely helpful. They include the National Library of Ireland, the National Archives, the Library of Trinity College, Dublin, and the Alumni Office of Trinity College, Dublin, the Library of the Church of Ireland Representative Body, the Imperial War Museum, the Oireachtas Library, the libraries of *The Irish Times* (especially Mr. John Gibson), the *Irish Independent*, the *Irish Press* (especially Mr. Brian Barron), *The Sunday Tribune* and *The Western People*.

Finally my thanks go to my publisher, Mr. John O'Connor of Blackwater Press, for inviting me to write the book, and to Ms. Anna O'Donovan, Senior Editor there, for seeing the book skilfully and safely into production.

MARY ROBINSON

The Life and Times of an Irish Liberal

1

THE BOURKES

At five o'clock in the evening on Thursday 27 May 1993, a lone bugler of the Grenadier Guards sounded a salute outside Buckingham Palace. His regimental colleagues formed an honour guard as the seventh President of Ireland, Mary Robinson, was greeted by Sir Robert Fellowes, private secretary to Queen Elizabeth II. The President was ushered to the Audience Room of the palace and the history of Anglo-Irish relations was about to witness a significant entry in its turbulent pages.

Another history - that of the President's family - was also witnessing an updating. Just six days after her 49th birthday, Mary Robinson became the first President of Ireland to be received at Buckingham Palace. She was not, however, the first of her family to be received there or to have connections with the Royal Household.

Ireland's seventh President is a Bourke of Ballina, Co. Mayo.

Bourkes of one ilk or another have been in Mayo since the thirteenth century. Bourke, Burke or de Burgh is one of the most common Hiberno-Norman surnames. The first of that family bearing that name to come to Ireland did so with the Norman Invasion and was granted lands in Connacht. They settled down, as the historian Edward McLysaght observes, to become more completely Irish than most other Norman families. They accepted Irish laws and customs and became Irish chieftains in their own right. Many of their descendants still populate Ballina and other parts of that corner of Ireland which Cromwell offered the native Irish as an alternative to Hell.

3

Mary Robinson was born Marie Terese Winifred Bourke on 21 May 1944 in that West of Ireland market town of Ballina. Her parents, Aubrey de Vere Bourke and Tessa Bourke, were both medical doctors. Aubrey Bourke had a flourishing medical practice in the town. He had been educated by the Jesuits at Mount St. Mary's in England before studying medicine at Edinburgh University where a relative was a medical Fellow. Tessa Bourke was born Tessa O'Donnell, in the Inishowen Peninsula in Co. Donegal, to Hubert and Winifred O'Donnell. There were six children in the O'Donnell family, four of whom became doctors. Tessa was a medical graduate of University College Dublin and before marrying Aubrey Bourke she had practised medicine in the Aran Islands in the 1930s. She was an immensely popular woman at the University, where she was a keen hockey player.

Mary was the third of her five children and the only girl in the family. One of the most significant influences on the life of the young Mary Bourke was her paternal grandfather, Henry Charles Bourke, known in Ballina, even 30 years after his death, only by his first initials H.C. He was a prominent Co. Mayo solicitor who commenced practice in the town soon after qualifying in 1897. He too had come under the influence of another lawyer in the family. He had been apprenticed to his uncle, a formidable Mayo solicitor, Robert Paget Bourke.

Robert Paget Bourke's legal career had spanned the greater part of the nineteenth century. As a student at Mr. William's school in Ballina's Arthur Street he earned a reputation for his skill with his fists. Contemporary accounts recall him as a man who remained in all aspects of his personal and professional life a fighter, who rarely gave in to an opponent.

A memoir of those Ballina days by a school contemporary, the author and publisher Richard Joynt, recalls that he willingly took on all challengers. That attitude was carried over into his business affairs. Together with a prominent member of the local landed gentry, Col. Henry Knox-Gore, he vehemently opposed the Towns Improvement Act of 1854. Ballina was one of the first towns to adopt that measure which put a heavier tax burden on the owners of property. Commercial

4

directories for the period show Robert Paget Bourke as the owner of substantial property interests in and around Ballina.

Though formidable and frosty of manner, according to Joynt's account, he had a reputation for not walking away from his responsibilities. The Church of Ireland Baptismal Register in Ballina records an illegitimate son, James, born to him in 1864. Unlike so many upper-middle-class men of his day, he did not turn tail from the situation; he gave the child his own name and made sure his needs and those of the mother were seen to.

After Henry Charles qualified as a solicitor he joined his uncle's, Robert Paget Bourke's practice which was then in John Street, Ballina. He later established his own practice in Ballina. H.C. Bourke married Eleanor Dorothy Macaulay in 1905. She was an extremely devout Roman Catholic who had considered becoming a nun but at the insistence of her father, Dr. Roger Macaulay, she abandoned the idea in favour of marriage.

To establish a family home H.C. Bourke purchased the leasehold, and later the freehold, of part of the Jones Estate in Ballina which included an imposing low-fronted eighteenth century house which he called Amana. It was here that Mary Robinson's father, Aubrey Bourke grew up.

The house is in the shadow of the place of worship of Ballina's Church of Ireland community - the charming eighteenth century St. Michael's - where many Bourke relatives are buried. Early maps of Ballina name the house as Ardnaree House. It was one of the earliest unfortified houses in Connacht and is described in the period 1783-1820 in a diary kept by Miss Elizabeth Ham, the daughter of an English merchant prince who settled in Ballina and whose home it was for a period.

H.C. Bourke and Eleanor Macaulay had seven children. The eldest, born in 1906, was given the Christian name Paget, after the family of that name into which Henry Charles Bourke's grandfather had married. The other children were Ivy, who graduated from Trinity College Dublin, joined the Sacred Heart Order and spent 50 years of her life as a nun in India; Hal, who became a doctor and practised as a GP in the town of Lydd in Kent before retiring to the South of France; next came Aubrey, Mary Robinson's father, followed by Roddy who was an officer in the RAF before moving to live in Australia, where amongst other business interests he had a chain of cinemas. The next born was Dorothy who joined the Order of Jesus and Mary straight from school. The last born was Denis who left TCD to write and act in plays, some of which made it to the West End in London. He abandoned the theatre for the world of business and later moved to live in South America.

Their father Henry Charles Bourke had a passionate interest in racing. He kept a stable of racehorses and hunters. He owned a winner of one of Ireland's premier races, the Punchestown Cup, a horse called Macadas, and he also had a winner of the prestigious Galway Plate. One of his most successful racehorses was named Nellie Mac after his wife. Another of his stable, The Whip, was a popular and successful performer at local point-to-point races in Mayo and Galway. His wife, Eleanor, known in the family as Nellie, was one of the first women in Ireland to become Master of Fox Hounds. The hounds of the North Mayo Harriers, with which the family hunted, were kennelled at H.C. Bourke's house, Amana.

Henry Charles was not a republican but he was a nationalist who retained a certain sympathy for the Empire.

Depending on whom one speaks to in Ballina one will be told that his house was raided for guns and cars by the IRA or by the Black and Tans. Like most solicitors of his background, he was wise enough to see the wind of change and he appeared at the Sinn Féin courts which were set up as an alternative to the administration of British justice in Ireland in the period before independence.

For his trouble he was charged before a Field General Court-Martial on 28 January 1921 where he pleaded not guilty to a charge of having taken part in the proceedings of a Republican Court at Belmullet, Co. Mayo, on 19 October 1920. He was also charged with being in possession of Republican summonses which, as the charge put it, were "likely to cause disaffection".

In his defence his King's Counsel, Mr. Price, said his client was a prominent solicitor who had practised for 24 years in the county. A Co. Mayo magistrate swore that he knew Mr. Bourke had addressed various recruiting meetings during the Great War. His Counsel said H.C. Bourke had lost his seat on the old Mayo County Council because he was "not on the Sinn Féin ticket".

The matter was settled by a stiff fine and an even stiffer warning.

Henry Charles had married into a wealthy Co. Mayo medical family. The Macaulays were prominent and prosperous enough in Co. Mayo at the end of the nineteenth century for them to be in a position to donate a stained glass window to Ballina's Roman Catholic Cathedral in time for the building's dedication in 1893. The window shows the highly idealised sacerdotal figures of St. Patrick and St. Bridget and its inscription asks the passing worshipper to pray for the donors, Dr. and Mrs. Macaulay.

When Henry Charles Bourke married Eleanor Macaulay her father, Roger, had one of the most substantial medical practices in the West of Ireland. He drove one of the first motor cars to appear on the pot-holed roads of the West; he kept a vast telescope which he would roll out on to the street to pursue his passion for amateur astronomy, and, like his son-in-law, he had a keen interest in horses.

One of that family, Thomas A. Macauley, was a member of the Irish Republican Brotherhood and an activist in the Mayo Land League. He was sentenced to ten years penal servitude in Mountjoy Jail in Dublin for his part in what became known as the "Crossmolina Conspiracy". He and six others were alleged to have conspired to kill a landlord's agent in Co. Mayo. All seven were the victims of informers' evidence which was used to convict them when the case came before Cork Assizes in 1883.

In the nineteenth century the marriages made by the Bourkes followed no rigid religious pattern. Some of the family married into their own Church, the Church of Ireland, others married Roman Catholics. Religion really only became a problem for the family in the

7

twentieth century. However, the Bourkes invariably married well.

It was through one of those marriages that the Bourke family came to have a tradition of service in the colonies of the British Empire, both in the army and in the Crown legal administration.

That service became most notable after the marriage of John Bourke of Heathfield House, Ballycastle, Co. Mayo to Elizabeth Paget in 1815. Elizabeth Paget was a member of a family of Co. Mayo, landed gentry who had two family seats in Co. Mayo, at Knockglass near Crossmolina and at Kinard near Enniscrone. Several members of those branches of the Paget family served as Justices of the Peace and others were career army men. They were cousins of the Paget family who had been created Earls of Uxbridge and Marquesses of Anglesey.

Two of the principal routes for the social advancement of the middle-class in nineteenth century Ireland were through the Church and the Army. Elizabeth Paget Bourke chose the latter route for three of her sons. She was well connected both in Dublin Castle from where British rule was administered in Ireland, and in the Viceregal Lodge where, by a curious coincidence, Mary Robinson now lives. Family lore has it that Elizabeth Paget Bourke had her coachman drive her from Mayo to the Viceregal Lodge where she used her influence with the then Viceroy, her kinsman Henry William Paget, Marquis of Anglesey, so that he might find commissions in the Army for her sons. She acquired commissions for her sons William Orme Paget Bourke, Oliver Paget Bourke, and Paget John Bourke.

William Orme Paget Bourke, the great-grandfather of Mary Robinson, was a captain in the 18th Regiment of Foot. He served with the regiment in various garrison postings in Ireland. The 18th of Foot or Royal Irish Regiment was one of the oldest independent garrison regiments raised in Ireland. It was founded by the Earl of Granard in 1684.

William married Jane Morrogh in 1856 thus strengthening family ties with the landed gentry but also bringing about its conversion to Catholicism. The girls of that marriage were brought up as Protestants,

8

the boys as Catholics. One family story has it that the decision to do so was made on the toss of a coin. However, it is more likely that Jane Morrogh insisted that the boys be brought up as Roman Catholics.

Jane Morrogh was the daughter of Henry Morrogh of Rathcooney, Co. Cork whose family were old Catholic gentry. An ancestor, Thomas Morrogh, when High Sheriff of Cork, received King James II in the city on 12 March 1689. James, who was making a hasty retreat from his problems in England, presented Morrogh, not with the Jacobite title he was expecting from the embattled Catholic monarch, but with a rosary. That rosary is still held by the head of the senior branch of the family now resident in Argentina.

By the time his son Henry Charles was born in 1875, William Orme Paget Bourke had left the army. At that time the family lived outside the Co. Mayo village of Bunniconlon in a house called Oatlands - a solid three-bay Georgian house overlooking the broad sweep of the Ox Mountains.

It fell not to William but to his brother, Oliver Paget Bourke, to bring military distinction to the family.

Lt. General Oliver Paget Bourke is commemorated with an impressive memorial tablet in St. Michael's Church of Ireland, Ballina. He obtained his first commission in the British Army as Ensign in the 17th Regiment in 1835. He served with the 17th during the campaign of 1838-9 in Afghanistan and Baluchistan. He was present at the storming of Chuznee and the capture of Khelat in 1839 under General Lord Keane. He saw service in the Crimea and was present at the Siege of Sevastopol in command of his Regiment from December 1854 to February 1855. Later, with the rank of Colonel, he served as Exon of the Queen's Royal Bodyguard and was promoted Major General in 1873. He retired to Ireland with the rank of Lt. General and died in Kingstown (Dun Laoghaire) in April 1880.

The General's other brother, Paget John Bourke, was a captain in the Household Cavalry. He was a great favourite of Queen Victoria and served as part of her Royal Bodyguard. She presented him with a diamond ring for one of his brides. The Captain married three times, and rather well on each of those occasions, amassing a considerable personal fortune by the standard of those times. For some years he had an apartment in Buckingham Palace but his main residence was an impressive house at St. Edmund's Terrace, Regent's Park. His heir was his favourite nephew, Mary Robinson's grandfather, Henry Charles Bourke.

Another family connection to Victoria's Court was made through another Paget cousin, Sir James Paget, a medical graduate of Trinity College Dublin, who was surgeon to the Queen.

Military and colonial connections were maintained by the family late into this century. A Bourke relative through marriage, Lt. Col. Joseph George Morrogh Bernard, had a distinguished military career which saw him wounded in action in World War I, and serving in World War II in France, and the Middle East. He was part of the GI "101" Mission which took Emperor Haile Selassie back to Abyssinia from the Sudan.

In this century the Bourke family maintained the link with the colonial service through Mary Robinson's uncle, Sir Paget John Bourke. He was knighted by Queen Elizabeth II in 1957 after a distinguished career as a Judge in the Colonial Service. Sir Paget served in some of the last outposts of Empire, amongst them Palestine, Kenya, Gibraltar and Cyprus.

He married Susan Killeen, the daughter of Michael Killeen the County Registrar for Co. Clare. He proposed to her by telegram from the Seychelles and the engagement ring he gave her was the ring given by Queen Victoria to Captain Paget John Bourke.

Sir Paget's name had appeared on the death lists of freedom fighters in Palestine and in Cyprus. His son, John Bourke, recalls how in Cyprus his father was protected by two personal bodyguards while his home was guarded by a platoon of soldiers. He remained unscathed until he retired to his Dublin home, 10 Herbert Park, where he was kidnapped on the afternoon of 30 April 1975. There was speculation at the time that he might have been exchanged for the imprisoned republican activist, Dr. Rose Dugdale, who was then on hunger strike in Limerick jail. There was also speculation that he was taken in error and that the intended victim was the then British Ambassador to Ireland, Sir Andrew Gilchrist. Sir Paget was released unharmed after less than a day with his captors.

Being prosperous, and with what was seen locally as a Big House background, it is not surprising that in the Ballina of the early 1940s, when Ireland was but 20 years independent, the Bourkes were looked on by many in much the same way as the Anglo-Irish planters were - with a curious mixture of respect and not a little envy. The description "elitist, rugby-playing hooray Henrys" has been used by local people in very recent times to describe the Bourkes. Even today in Ballina, when the subject of the Bourke's family history is mentioned, there is, at the very least, some residual unease about the colonial connections. But for the most part Mary Robinson's election as President of Ireland has swept much of that attitude aside.

When she was establishing her reputation as a young senator even the most liberal of publications could not resist a dig at Mary Robinson's background. In 1974, a short-lived Dublin publication called *Man Alive* presented this view of the Bourkes of Ballina in a profile of Mary Robinson:

"Local people claim the family finds its spiritual home far from Ireland, and that its services to the British Empire are more noteworthy than its services to Ireland."

In a republican heartland like Ballina such a view would be quite natural. The motto on the family tomb in St. Michael's in Ballina is hardly likely to endear the memory of those resting there to the majority of the townspeople. It reads: "One King, One Faith, One Law."

Sir Paget Bourke's service on the colonial bench and the fact that his mother and brother, Aubrey, attended at Buckingham Palace when he was knighted is still remembered in Ballina with a degree of unease. Some older members of the Irish Bar recall that on his return to practise in Ireland, some colleagues used the tag "West Brit" and "Castle Catholic" to describe Sir Paget Bourke as he went about his business in the Four Courts. But such a view of him is dismissed by other former colleagues at the Irish Bar. The author and barrister, Charles Lysaght, remembers Mary Robinson's uncle as "very much an Irishman who sent his sons home to Ireland to school at Clongowes Wood". John Bourke recalled how his father was very much aware of his Irishness, especially on his foreign postings, where he and other Irish members of the Colonial Service were seen "very much as Irishmen".

He was a type of Irishman that one seldom finds now, except perhaps in the rarefied atmosphere of one of Dublin's gentlemen's clubs or perhaps in the pages of a Molly Keane novel.

Colonial, legal and military connections in the Bourke family extended beyond the career of Sir Paget. Mary Robinson's great-aunt Muriel, Lady Sheridan, was married to Sir Joseph Sheridan of Spencer Park, Castlebar, Co. Mayo. Born Muriel Macaulay she was the fourth daughter of Dr. Roger Macaulay, into whose family Mary Robinson's grandfather, H.C. Bourke, had married. Sir Joseph was educated at Castleknock College and Trinity College Dublin. He was called to the Irish Bar in 1907 and joined the British Colonial Service a year later. He became Chief Justice of Kenya and President of the Court of Appeal of Eastern Africa. He also chaired the controversial Masai Riots Claims Commission in 1918-9. A deeply religious man, he was known in the family as "holy Joe".

There were few visible signs of ostentation attached to the way the Bourkes lived in Ballina. Their life-style was not grand. Aubrey and Tessa Bourke were not particularly fond of foreign travel. According to their son Adrian they went occasionally to Cheltenham for the races or Wimbledon for the tennis. The children were sent to good Roman Catholic boarding schools and to Trinity College Dublin. They had ponies to ride. There was a nanny and domestic help. In rural Ireland of the '40s and '50s domestic servants' wages were not high and in the West they were lower than in most other parts of the country. The overall impression of the Bourke household is one of professional prosperity, stoutly aided by certain judicious house property

12

interests and land acquisitions in and around Ballina.

Conscious, no doubt, of how his family might be perceived if his sister's bid for the presidency were successful, Henry Bourke wrote in the *Sunday Tribune* during the election campaign that the family's prosperity was relevant only in that it instilled in them from an early age that they "owed more to society".

The family lived above Dr. Bourke's surgery in a comfortable and impressive three-storey house on Victoria Terrace. Some townspeople point out that the house should bear the address Emmet Terrace, the name by which it is known locally, but the Bourkes have always called it by its older name.

Flanked by the town's two principal bridges, Victoria House has a pleasant aspect, facing the broad expanse of the river Moy and the impressive façade of St. Muredach's Cathedral. That part of Ballina is rich in history. In the eighteenth century, Arthur Young, in his *Tour in Ireland*, records how impressed he was with that particular part of the town, which then contained the house and magnificent gardens of Col. Henry King.

While the front façade of the Bourkes' house faces on to the Moy, one side backs on to Lloyd's Lane which runs from the relative calm of the river to busy Pearse Street. In the plot of land behind the house - now a bank car park - a United Irishman is reputed to have been hanged by the British after the 1798 Rebellion. At the top of Lloyd's Lane stands the Moy Hotel with its Gothic front facing on to the former Knox Street (now Pearse Street). The building was the Bourkes' townhouse in the early nineteenth century. Its chipped and faded elegance is a sad reminder of a more leisurely time in Ballina's history. George Bernard Shaw was a guest here, as was Maud Gonne. From the balcony of the hotel Charles Stewart Parnell addressed the citizens of the town and the county in 1891.

From one of the tall, elegant Georgian windows at the rear of her Ballina home the young Mary Bourke could see the spot from where Parnell addressed the faithful in 1891. Ballina had remained loyal to Parnell during the divisive Parnellite split of that year.

When Dr. Bourke purchased the Victoria Terrace house it did not have a garden. He later bought a nearby plot which he cultivated himself. The children used Lloyd's Lane as a playground. The grounds of their grandfather's house, Amana, elegantly perched overlooking the town of Ballina, provided them with a place to ride their ponies, often under the watchful eye of John Timlan, H.C.'s farm manager.

The principal streets of Ballina slope down to the river Moy. The town developed on the west side of the river in the eighteenth century under the patronage of, amongst others, O'Hara Lord of Tyrawley. Towards the end of that century Ballina had made its mark on Irish history by becoming the second town taken by the French expeditionary force under the command of General Humbert. His defeat and surrender to the British was a bitter blow to the aspirations of the town's citizens.

It was in this historic market town that the future President of Ireland spent the first ten years of her life. Cosseted in the comforting and supportive web of her prosperous professional family she saw and experienced little of the considerable poverty of her West of Ireland neighbours.

Early family photographs invariably show a smiling, confident girl who was certain of her family's love and the devotion of a doting nanny, Co. Mayo woman Anne Coyne, from Knockmore near Ballina. Like all nannies she played a pivotal role in the lives of her charges. She moved to Dublin when the Bourke children were at Trinity College, Dublin, and later became nanny to the Robinson children.

While those early photographs show Mary as confident, they also reveal her as a young girl capable of being tough, and this is the portrait of the young girl that friends remember. A neighbour from Victoria Terrace, Michael Durcan, remembers that "she was able to hold her own in football with the young boys of the street". Joseph McDonnell, a lecturer at the National College of Art and Design, who was also a Ballina neighbour, remembers her wearing an impressive cowboy outfit complete with six-guns. "She was," he recalled, "a tomboy and great fun." Adrian Bourke remembers how conscious his sister was of the need to prove that she could achieve anything that the boys in the family could achieve. This became more obvious when the tomboy got an opportunity to display her intellectual skills in the school classroom.

2

A PRIVATE EDUCATION

Mary Bourke's early education was not at any of Ballina's national schools, but at Miss Claire Ruddy's private preparatory school, at Ardnaree on the east side of the river Moy. The school had the advantage of being near the family home. A short stroll along the Moy's bank, leaving behind the crumbling ruin of a fourteenth century Augustinian priory, a bracing walk over Thomas Ham bridge, passing Ballina Flour Mills within earshot of the river's roaring weir, and Mary Bourke found herself at Miss Ruddy's academy.

There the children of the burghers of Ballina were prepared for entrance to the private boarding schools that would finally separate many of them from their parents and from Ballina. They were also spared any association with what some class-conscious parents may have considered undesirable local children; the unfortunates immortally dubbed by James Joyce's father as "Paddy stink and Mickey muck."

Dorothy McKane was one of the last students to attend the Ballina private school before it closed its doors in 1969. She remembers its headmistress Miss Ruddy as an "independent-minded woman who was an ultra nationalist". She had a particular fondness for the Irish language and for the classics. Ballina had had several such private schools which came and went with the changing fortunes of the nineteenth and early twentieth centuries. Even long after Irish independence many such private preparatory schools in rural Ireland were run by Unionist matriarchs. Claire Ruddy, however, was an ardent Roman Catholic nationalist in the somewhat romantic tradition of Maud Gonne. Her young charges may not have seen her in quite such a sympathetic light. Adrian Bourke, Mary Robinson's brother, remembers the schoolmistress as being "deadly accurate with the crack of a cane".

Contemporaries at Miss Ruddy's remember the young Mary Bourke as more outgoing than her brothers. One recalls her as being more interested in boys' games than in the stereotypical dolls-house activities of her female classmates. Her brother Henry remembers the rough and tumble of playing Batman and Robin with his older sister. "Mary was very fair about sharing the roles," he recalled many years later. "A burgeoning sense of justice, perhaps?"

From the earliest years at Miss Ruddy's her academic progress was invariably registered as exceptional - a pattern that was to be maintained for the rest of her academic career.

Mary Bourke's sense of belonging to the West of Ireland and to Ballina was questioned during her public career. Her second-ever utterance in the Senate was at once a declaration and defence of her origins. "On a point of order," the young Trinity senator told the House, "I am from Mayo."

The remark was made to correct Senator Thomas P. Flanagan who, in a speech on the 1969 Appropriation Bill, grouped Mary Bourke with a clique of senators whom he claimed had a "city bias in regard to rural Ireland".

The senator from Ballina was not impressed. Nor was Senator Flanagan convinced. His retort, "By birth, yes," suggests that he felt there was need of further proof of the Senator's umbilical link, as it were, to the West of Ireland and to the town of Ballina. She told Christina Murphy in an interview in *The Irish Times* in 1977, that she has "a deep sense of being a Mayo woman, over and above anything else". She spoke about how the local people saw her as Mary Bourke a native of the town and not as Mary Robinson the senator. Christina Murphy, herself a Mayo woman, remarked how she saw Mary Robinson as differing from her fellow county-women, in that what she remembers most of Mayo is a happy family life and not the poverty and deprivation around her. But those would be issues for later times.

18

Dr. Aubrey Bourke has recalled how close his daughter was to her mother. "Her mother encouraged Mary to study law and also encouraged her in sport. When she died in 1973 it shattered her a lot," her father recalled. That was to be expected given that her mother made a special point of being on hand for all the major events of her daughter's life, save one rather important one - her only daughter's wedding.

Dr. Tessa Bourke is remembered by friends as having had a strong, dominant personality. The writer and critic, Desmond McAvock, remembers her asking him to accommodate a Sheridan relative of the family who was coming up to Trinity. She announced the idea to McAvock with a tag to the request, which went, "You must put him up, he's the last of the Sheridans!"

She had a passion for fine clothes, particularly the work of the designer Mary O'Donnell. She drove a Ford Zodiac at great speed to and from Dublin to see her children at Trinity. She encouraged her sons' interest in rugby and other sports. Her son Adrian remembers her enjoying conjuring up notional Irish rugby sides, over a drink in the Shelbourne Hotel's Horseshoe Bar, with former Irish rugby international and Heinz Corporation chairman Tony O'Reilly. She played so central a role in her children's lives that nearly 20 years after her death her son Henry said both father and children felt they had lost the essence of the family, or as Adrian Bourke put it, "the heartland of all our lives had terminated".

Three years after her mother's death her daughter said she still found it hard to talk about it and she kept getting the feeling that she would have so very much loved to have been able to show her mother her own children.

Mary Bourke's first real away-from-home experience began in 1954, when at the age of ten she left Ballina to board at Mount Anville School in Dublin. Mount Anville - administered by the nuns of the Society of the Sacred Heart - is situated in the solidly middle-class Dublin suburb of Dundrum. Like most Irish convent boarding schools in the 1950s, Mount Anville was an island community. It was the sort of school that insisted on putting a particular stamp on a young girl. Mary Bourke had the advantage of having an aunt who was a member of the Order and this was the family connection to Mount Anville.

In those days the Sacred Heart nuns were to girls' education what the Jesuits were to boys'. Mount Anville was set apart from the busy commercial heart of Dublin city. Nearby, in the nineteenth century, had lived the princes of Irish industry, whose houses and grounds were being bought up in the 1950s by the property developers of the new Ireland so that they might create the sprawling housing estates that have all but strangled that old part of Dublin.

At Mount Anville Mary Bourke was considered to be a genuine all-rounder. School records and year books indicate a good performance in all subjects and place her as slightly above average in sports. "In any year," Sister Joan Stephenson, her Mistress of Studies, recalls, "Mary Bourke would have been in the top three." Sr. Joan was impressed by her "great moral and intellectual integrity" and by the fact that while "a lot of people think within a framework", her student from Ballina "followed her own mind to an exceptional degree".

Sr. Joan also remembers Dr. and Mrs. Bourke at this time. "The Bourkes were not in any way a typical small-town family," she recalls, "though they were deeply involved in Ballina's life. There was a great breadth of outlook, a great culture and knowledge about them," the former Mistress of Studies says.

While Mary was at Mount Anville her four brothers, Oliver, Aubrey, Henry and Adrian were at James Joyce's old school, the Jesuit-run Clongowes Wood College in Co. Kildare. They were the second generation of Bourke boys to be educated at Clongowes. Though they met only on holidays and school Open Days the Bourke children remained close to one another.

A photograph of the seven family members at an Open Day at Clongowes in the late '50s, shows the very essence of middle-class prosperity; the boys smartly turned out in cricket flannels and college blazers, flanking mother, father and sister. With the ivy-clad neo-Gothic school buildings in the background, it could be a family photograph taken at any one of the great English public schools. It was light-years away from provincial Ballina.

Further evidence of family prosperity was Mary's attendance at a Paris finishing school in 1961-2. It had an unfortunate name, more akin to a Pigalle bordello than to a finishing school for young ladies. But Mademoiselle Anita's, at 10 rue l'Amiral d'Estaing, was one of the many polishing academies that Paris had to offer the daughters of the well-heeled. Sending girls to continental "finishing schools" was not unusual for upper middle class Irish Catholic families at that time.

Patience Ryan was a young Irish girl who attended Mlle. Anita's when Mary Bourke was a student there. Her most abiding memory of Mary at the school, and around Paris in the early '60s, is her fellow student's penchant for wearing the most impeccably starched white gloves when going out and about. She remembers Mlle. Anita Pojninska as "small, erect and very formidable", but she says she recalls the young Mary Bourke as "even more formidable than Mlle. Anita".

Patience Ryan remembers that the young Mary Bourke was held in awe by the other students because of her habit of engaging in intellectual arguments "which went over the heads of not just the other girls but the teachers as well".

"It seemed," Patience Ryan recalls, "that Mary Bourke had erected a fortress around her personality that was not easy to penetrate; she was very much in command and had very little tolerance for those who were not." Her intolerance also extended to the more promiscuous girls in the school. Over 30 years later Patience Ryan recalls that in Paris of the early '60s the young Mary Bourke "took a dim view of promiscuity".

The school no longer exists and 10 rue l'Amiral d'Estaing, where generations of young ladies perfected something akin to Nancy Mitford's code of "U and non U", is now the offices of the Bayard Press.

If Mary Bourke's attendance at Mlle. Anita's showed the dedication of the Bourkes to their daughter's advancement, so too did it show her willingness to advance. It also gave the future President an

21

advantage she would use to good effect many years later on her state visit to France as President of Ireland - total fluency in French and a deep understanding of French culture and literature.

Henry Bourke observed the change it wrought in his sister:

"A year in France completed the metamorphosis from tomboy to young woman, and I still have a crystal-clear memory of the moment when it occurred to me that this distinctly feminine creature who spoke fluent French along with some Italian and Spanish, who could intelligently discuss art and literature and current affairs, was lost forever as Batman... or Robin!"

3

TRINITY AND HARVARD

An ornate stone plaque on the front of a Regency house, 21 Westland Row, Dublin, commemorates the birth there of Oscar Wilde in 1854. Now the property of Wilde's first university, Trinity College, the house was the Bourkes' Dublin home for some years.

21 Westland Row, was modest by comparison with its grand eighteenth century neighbours in nearby Merrion Square, but very few Trinity undergraduates, even in those days, could aspire to such splendid accommodation in the capital.

The Bourke children lived together again in that house when all five were undergraduates at Trinity. The elder Bourke brothers, Oliver and Aubrey, followed their father's profession and read medicine; the younger brothers, Henry and Adrian, and their sister Mary, followed their grandfather's, and read law. When the Bourke children began their university education, the Catholic Church's ban on the attendance of the faithful at Trinity was still firmly in place.

The then Archbishop of Dublin, Dr. John Charles McQuaid, gave an audience to Dr. and Mrs. Bourke so that they might receive the archiepiscopal *imprimatur*, and have their children educated at Trinity without fear of any damage to their immortal souls. The Archbishop issued his prohibition on attendance at Trinity annually, at the beginning of Lent. It was included amongst a plethora of admonishments on such things as fasting and mixed marriages.

A year after Mary Bourke entered Trinity Dr. McQuaid advised in a Lenten pastoral that:

"The Church forbids parents and guardians to send a child to any non-Catholic school... or university. Deliberately to disobey this law is a mortal sin, and they who persist in disobedience are unworthy to receive the sacraments."

With their spiritual needs taken care of, Tessa Bourke, with a view to the physical needs of her children, arranged for the purchase of Sir William and Lady Wilde's old home, 21 Westland Row. It was perfectly located, close by the Lincoln Place gates of Trinity.

Mrs. Bourke also installed Nanny Coyne in the house to look after her Ballina charges. She furnished the main rooms in a style not entirely different from how they would have appeared in the Wildes' period of residence. Some Victorian furniture came from Ballina; the rest she acquired in Dublin. In those days a great many of Trinity's undergraduates lived in college rooms and the remainder lived in flats or lodgings. The Bourkes' domestic arrangements in Dublin were certainly far grander than those of many of their Trinity contemporaries. Very few undergraduates had live-in domestic help. Nanny Coyne was a superb cook and the house was run with great style and flair.

Only a decade before Mary Bourke matriculated, just 34 per cent of Trinity's students came from the South of Ireland. Northern students made up 18 percent of the student population and the rest came from Britain and overseas. One view of the college in the 1960s is clear from a remark quoted by Professor Denis Donoghue in a review article in the *London Review of Books* in August 1982. When Professor Donoghue pointed out to the President of University College Dublin that the *per capita* grant from the government to Trinity exceeded the grant to any of the colleges of the National University, the President dismissed his protestations. Trinity, the President of UCD said, was an irrelevance to Ireland and its development; it was merely an appendix to the country; the future of the country was in the hands of those who were being educated at UCD and they would win without the sherry, the Trinity Ball or the Elizabethan Society.

Trinity College, Dublin, in the 1960s had not been hit by the tidal wave of radical student revolt then sweeping all before it in American

24

and continental European universities. Apart from the occasional bit of banner-waving by the odd token "red", Trinity had retained much of its Oxbridge character and was still a leisurely place to be an undergraduate.

"In Trinity, at this time," Dr. Paul O'Grady recalls, "one still read for a degree, while across St. Stephen's Green at UCD they studied for a degree. And that, in those days," declares the Vienna-based history professor, "was the difference between the two universities!"

It would be an inaccurate picture of Trinity, in Mary Bourke's undergraduate years, to portray it as a place where the winds of change were not beginning to stir. The Board of the College had accepted two student nominees as non-voting members, and by the end of the decade women were appointed to the male preserve of Fellowship. But when Mary Bourke won her entrance scholarship to Trinity in 1963 only one woman had sat on the Board of the College.

The majority of Trinity undergraduates in the 1960s were politically conservative. There was one group, however, that Mary Bourke's generation would recall as perhaps the most colourful of the college's political activists. The Internationalists were a Maoist revolutionary forum, led not as one might have expected, by Trinity's working-class students, but by English public schoolboys. Their respect for freedom of speech was such that Brian Lenihan, when addressing a college meeting as a Government minister in the late '60s, had to make good his escape from them through a narrow lavatory window. The defenestration of a Government minister was the Internationalists' finest hour.

Senator David Norris remembers Trinity at the time as a college known for its "clubs, cravats, light sports cars and great champagne breakfasts". He remembers Mary Bourke in that atmosphere as a woman with a natural reserve and with "intellectual commitment" unusual for a woman in Trinity at the time. That intellectual commitment was to the study of law. The law was to become and to remain the main focus of her intellectual life at Trinity and beyond.

When Mary Bourke entered Trinity's Law School it was still

conservative by European standards. Traditionally it serviced Ireland's professional legal bodies - the Incorporated Law Society and the King's Inns. The Irish judiciary counted many Trinity graduates amongst their number, as did the British Colonial Service. It was not the sort of department that produced an abundance of liberals and free thinkers. Apart from the recent appointment of a South African anti-apartheid activist called Kadar Asmal, the staff of Trinity's Law School in the early '60s were mainly solid career academics.

The mostly male students of the law at the college (there were two other women in Mary Bourke's class) followed a predictable path into one or other branch of legal practice in Ireland or abroad. That is what TCD's Law School would have expected of Mary Bourke. All the indications were that that expectation would be fulfilled. She is remembered by staff and students as being serious about her studies, not especially interested in politics or frenetic socialising.

If anything, at this time, she was opposed to organisations and people with a trendy progressive tag. She had more in common with Trinity's future exponents of the Fine Gael Just Society than with the Labour Party. In talking to contemporaries from Trinity days it is the image of the "bluestocking" which comes across again and again.

The Law Society and the Students Representative Council, were amongst her main outlets in the college's social round. She spoke regularly at college debates, overcoming a natural shyness which dogged her most of her life, making her appear, at times, severe and socially aloof. A male admirer of the time remembers her at Trinity for her habit of wearing elegant full-length silk evening gloves while speaking at the more formal debates. Echoes perhaps, of Mademoiselle Anita's!

She said of college debating that it gave her an exhilarating feeling to have a hold over an audience and she enjoyed pitching her skills against her opponents in the bearpit of undergraduate debate.

Her list of college society attainments is solid rather than spectacular. She was Auditor of the Law Society, Secretary of the Students Representative Council and Editor of the student law review *Justice*. The college press records her as a competent if somewhat humourless debater. She debated in the final of the *Irish Times* debating competition and represented Trinity in *University Challenge* in Manchester where they lost to Somerville College, Oxford. In her senior freshman year she was elected to Scholarship - Trinity's highest undergraduate academic distinction.

At Trinity she met a Dubliner called Nicholas Kenneth Robinson. He was also reading law and in her law class. They soon became friends but only started dating towards the end of their student days.

At Trinity Nick Robinson's girlfriends included Ruth Buchanan, the RTE broadcaster now married to Senator Shane Ross. She was the daughter of Alfred Buchanan, Church of Ireland Dean of Kildare.

They dated for two years. She remembers Nick Robinson as a warm-hearted, generous young man. He took her to places most students couldn't afford: dinners at the Red Bank Restaurant, leisurely meals in Bernardos Italian restaurant near Trinity's Lincoln Place gate. Favourite drinking haunts included The Old Stand and Lincoln's Inn. They visited Nick's father in his flat in Merrion Street, which Ruth Buchanan especially remembers because it had a "wonderful collection of paintings by Jack B. Yeats".

"Nick was extremely generous," she recalls. "Once when I told him I was going to decorate a hat with fresh flowers for a Trinity Week garden party, he sent the most extravagant collection of flowers to my flat." She remembers Mary Bourke and her brothers at Trinity as somewhat strongly contrasting characters, with Mary being cast in the role of "something of a severe older sister".

Nick Robinson was a year younger than his future wife. He was the third of four boys in an upper middle-class Dublin Protestant family. Like the Bourkes, the Robinsons were financially secure. They came to Ireland in the seventeenth century from the North of England, settling first in the midlands and later in Dublin. One branch of Nick Robinson's family, with Sheffield origins, was appointed silversmiths to the Lord Lieutenant of Ireland in the early years of the reign of Queen Victoria. They worked from impressive business premises in Dame Street, adjacent to the frenetic social life which revolved around

Dublin Castle. In the late eighteenth century the Robinson family had been coopers and brewers in the Liberties - a part of the old city from where many coopers' workshops supplied barrels to the Guinness brewery.

Nick's father, Howard Waterhouse Robinson, was born in 1913. He graduated from Trinity and worked as a chartered accountant, founding the City of Dublin Bank, now the Anglo-Irish Bank Corp. He was closely associated with the Church of Ireland and through his accountancy practice looked after a great deal of its financial affairs. He was also a leading member of the Masonic Order.

Howard Robinson was the son of Ernest Robinson and Lilian Maud (known as Dolly) Waterhouse. Ernest Robinson joined the British Army and fought in the Boer War. He left the army to return to Ireland to look after the family coal business, only to abandon the business world again to return to army life with the Royal Army Service Corps.

Nick Robinson's mother, Lucy Macpherson Douglas, had studied at the College of Art in Kildare Street and her mother, Edith Collins, was a relative of the sculptor Foley whose statues of Burke and Goldsmith stand sentinel outside the West Front of Trinity College. Another of her relatives, a Lieutenant Reardon, was reputed to have been part of Napoleon's bodyguard on St. Helena.

The death of his mother in October 1956, when he was just ten years old, contributed to Nick Robinson's early independence. He was sent as a boarder to Mountjoy School. His quick wit made him popular with his school fellows. His popularity carried over to Trinity where, in the mood of the times, he was, as one friend recalled, "not one of the more serious academic types". While Mary Bourke sat at the front of the class frantically taking copious notes, Nick Robinson sat languidly at the back drawing cartoons of his lecturers and classmates.

After serving an apprenticeship with the Dublin solicitors, Matheson, Ormsby and Prentice, Nick Robinson decided to try his hand at being a professional cartoonist in London. He had already earned a reputation at Trinity and in his place of apprenticeship as something of a doodler. He was unsure at that time about going into full-time legal practice. He chose instead to have a bash in the uncertain world of the professional cartoonist.

He later worked as a political cartoonist for *The Irish Times*, of which newspaper his father was a director. The year was 1967 and the decade was swinging at its most outrageous.

If he was unsure about his life as a lawyer, there was one thing of which Robinson was absolutely certain in 1967. He had made up his mind to ask Mary Bourke to marry him. As in all the best student love stories, that was not to be - at least not for the present. For the time being, the law, which young Robinson had just abandoned, was to cause him to be abandoned in turn.

Mary Bourke, maintaining the trend established all those years before at Miss Ruddy's preparatory school in Ballina, had covered herself in academic distinction yet again. She took a first class Moderatorship (the B.A. Mod. in Legal Science) and a first class LL.B. While she was on the top rung of her year's academic ladder, Nick Robinson was on the bottom. He secured the last of the Third Class places that year. Mary Bourke crowned her distinctions by winning a scholarship to the prestigious Harvard Law School. She finished her finals at Trinity, spent a night on the town celebrating and took a flight to Boston the following day. She was ten days late for the start of term.

Nick Robinson and his girlfriend parted ways; he to the Beatlemania of late '60s London, she to the Vietnam-ridden hysteria of Ivy-League Boston; she with her string of "firsts"; he with a third-class degree. The suitor arrived at the door of 21 Westland Row the morning of Mary Bourke's departure for Harvard. He was carrying a single red rose. When the door was opened he found only Nanny Coyne - the family had already left for the airport. Nanny received the rose accompanied by the words, "If she can't have this I can't think of anyone else I'd rather give it to". Nanny Coyne, who had her instructions to keep all boyfriends well away from the house, always had a soft spot for Nick Robinson, and for him she made an exception to the house rules. She would sometimes see him while Mary was in Harvard and pass on her news of Mary's progress there.

Harvard, unlike Trinity, had not escaped the student revolution. What impressed the new arrival from complacent Trinity was the level and intensity of student involvement in public affairs. Harvard was to be the instrument of her Pauline conversion.

"There was intense questioning then," she recalls of her early days at Harvard. "I had a law degree, but I hadn't really been encouraged to think. And Harvard was just facing up to the fact that there were inequalities of sex and race."

The Harvard Law School had little in common with its Trinity counterpart. Academics there encouraged discussion. Central to their teaching methods was the business of examining the laws' unresolved ambiguities. The graduate of the Harvard Law School was as likely to become a civil rights activist as a major captain of industry or a legal practitioner. Mary Bourke left there in 1968 with far more than the LL.M she had come for. She was to publicly acknowledge her debt to Harvard many times. "The young people I met there," she told *The Irish Times* in 1977, "were much more prepared to accept responsibility; to seek and to want involvement."

"I found it a very exciting time," she told *The Chicago Tribune* in 1990. "I found that there was a great questioning of the values of society. It was the period of the Vietnam War and the civil rights movement in the South. There was even questioning of the teaching of the law and values of a legal education. Everything was up for examination."

The end of the Johnson era in America forced young American graduates to look at their country in a different light. Many of the more idealistic ones at Harvard were turning down large salaries offered by city legal firms, opting instead to get involved in civil rights campaigns. It was the era of the new approach.

Her one-year course at Harvard was intense and there was little time for socialising. Mary spent what free time she had at the theatre.

It was during this time that she developed a passion for contemporary drama.

Mary Bourke began to relate what she saw at Harvard to the situation in Ireland. She returned home transformed by her American experience. The "bluestocking" had had a conversion to liberalism and now she wanted to do something positive about it. She decided that her best avenue of approach was through what she knew best - the law. To pursue that end she decided not to remain in America, but to return to Ireland.

4

SENATOR MARY T.W. BOURKE

In the dying moments of the 1960s Mary Bourke's life was suddenly moving in several new directions all at once.

The Irish Times of 11 July 1969 announced that Mary T.W. Bourke, B.A.(Mod.), LL.B (Dubl.), LL.M.(Harvard), had been appointed by the Board of Trinity College Dublin to be Reid Professor in the Law School from which she had only recently graduated. The appointment of a 25-year-old woman to a Trinity law chair founded in 1888 surprised the academic legal establishment. To add further to that sense of surprise the same report in *The Irish Times* announced casually:

"Miss Bourke is a candidate on the Dublin University panel for the Senate."

She had no political experience whatsoever and her family on both sides had no particular involvement in party politics. Her only foray into college politics was her election as secretary of the Student Representative Council and one attendance at a Maoist meeting which she described as "sheer boredom".

It was the Harvard experience which prompted the quantum leap from apolitical, obscure provincial barrister to high profile Senate candidate. While the actual decision to stand may have come about as much by chance as by any preconceived plan, once it had been arrived at, Mary Bourke became a woman with a well thought-out career agenda.

A conversation with Trinity friends on her return from Boston literally changed the course of her life. During that conversation, in the summer of 1969, she made the point that if Trinity's presence in the Senate was to be effective in the future, the graduates could do worse than elect a young person. It did not take a great deal of encouragement for that group of friends to persuade Mary Bourke that she was that young person.

While she was not a reluctant candidate, she did do a certain amount of oracle consulting before finally letting her name go forward. She made a journey West for two reasons. The first was to consult a friend in Mayo, Canon Luce, whose opinions would be representative of Trinity's older Protestant graduates which then formed the bulk of the electorate. He gave her every encouragement.

Armed with his enthusiastic response she made her second consultation.

"I still remember my father's face when I told him," she told *The Irish Times* nearly 20 years after her election. "He was out digging in the garden in Ballina, and he leaned his elbow on the spade and looked at me for a very long while without saying anything."

Aubrey Bourke doubted that his daughter would be elected but far from discouraging her the whole family weighed in behind the campaign.

In 1969 someone of Mary Bourke's age faced one major problem in winning a Dublin University seat. The majority of the graduates who were eligible to vote were elderly and conservative. The goodwill of her Trinity contemporaries was encouraging but of little practical help. Many of them were ineligible to vote having failed to do such a simple thing as fill in the Senate registration form given to them on the day of graduation. All Irish citizens who are graduates of Trinity are entitled to vote in the Senate election but they are required to register to vote. Quite often in the excitement of the Commencements ceremony the registration forms get left behind.

The young candidate faced two other obstacles which she herself saw as serious blocks to her success. She was a woman and she was also a Catholic. She was not, as has often appeared in print, the first woman to stand for the Trinity panel. Charlotte Lane McClenaghan stood in 1954 and in 1957, but failed to get elected. Frances-Jane French also stood in 1957 but polled only 46 votes. The omens were not good.

That summer of 1969, 21 Westland Row became campaign head-quarters. Her brother Adrian enlisted the aid of his friends. He asked a dynamic young Cork woman, Ann Lane from Millstreet, to administer the office. She did so with such skill and success that nearly a quarter of a century later she is still with Mary Robinson in Áras an Uachtaráin.

Mary took as her election agent the inspired choice of Trevor West, then a lecturer and Assistant Junior Dean at Trinity. While West would have been seen in some circles as part of the Protestant establishment, such things sat lightly on his shoulders. He was immensely popular in a wide range of college circles, especially with the sporting bucks. His father was the Headmaster of Midleton College in Co. Cork and through that connection he knew generations of Co. Cork Trinity graduates.

He was well placed to canvass votes from a wide circle of Trinity graduates. Later he too was to represent Trinity in the Senate.

The campaign to elect Mary Bourke was a new departure from the old style Trinity campaigns which were more like the mysterious Masonic process which elects members of a gentlemen's club. Mary Bourke was standing on serious issues.

A bold manifesto to the Trinity electorate of 6,625 voters named the platforms on which she stood. According to her first heading she stood "As a Young Person". Under that heading she told the electorate that she would express "with energy and vigour the views of a younger generation aware of the vital part Trinity plays in the intellectual life of the country". Under that heading she also trotted out the safe view that the merger of TCD and UCD, proposed by the late Donagh O'Malley when Minister for Education, would be a backward step for Trinity.

She offered herself to the electorate under a second heading "As a Liberal". Just how liberal she was in those days is not really evident from this section of the manifesto. This was no doubt a wise move, given that the constituency of Dublin University with its one constituent college, Trinity, was not made up of a particularly liberal body of people at that time.

The candidate expressed dissatisfaction with what she called "a tendency to feel self-satisfied south of the border" in relation to the fight for civil liberties in Northern Ireland. Given her largely Protestant constituency she made brave reference to the success of the Second Vatican Council in promoting pluralist values. The young liberal also advocated reform of the law where it constrained individual liberty without the justification of preserving public order or promoting the safety of the State.

Under the heading "As a Lawyer" she told the electorate that if she won a seat she would have both the time and the enthusiasm to "review extensively the content and scope of legislation before the Senate". Reminding her voters that she had "no strong political affiliation" she said she would be guided only by "a patriotic idealism".

Finally she offered herself for election "As a Woman". Here was no bold feminist statement. Playing a low-key approach she merely said that the more women were ready to "branch out" the more doors will open "in the face of quiet ability and feminine qualities of efficiency and good humour". This was a statement hardly likely to appeal to any staunch late '60s feminists in the electorate.

She ended her manifesto with an appeal for first preference votes from "the young and the older generations who are young at heart".

Reading the manifesto 24 years after it was written, it appears both dated and safe. To the Trinity electorate of 1969 it came as a breath of fresh air. The intellectual calibre of Trinity representatives in the Irish Senate and the quality of their contribution to debates in the Upper House could not be faulted. But for the most part they were what W.B. Yeats called "smiling public men" who were more concerned with their academic affairs than with public life. That is what Mary Bourke was now offering to change.

In her attempt to do just that she did not lack support amongst Trinity's Protestant and Catholic establishment, within and without the college walls. Her proposer was Professor C.B. McKenna, Regius Professor of Laws and her seconder was Howard Robinson, Nick Robinson's father. Amongst her nominators and supporters were the Archbishop of Dublin, Dr. George Otto Simms; the Bishop of Tuam, the Rt. Rev. Arthur Butler; the Dean of Kildare, Rev. A.D. Buchanan; the poet and scholar Prof. Brendan Kennelly; the poet Eavan Boland; the political scientist Prof. Basil Chubb; the Lady McDermott; the Medieval historian, Prof. Annette Jocelyn Otway-Ruthven; and the historian Prof. T.W. Moody. There was also a liberal sprinkling of well-known solicitors and barristers - the addition of whose names would guarantee a good proportion of the legal vote.

When the votes were counted in the Public Theatre of Trinity College on 12 August 1969, the first count returned the outgoing senators Owen Sheehy Skeffington and W.J.E. Jessop. The other outgoing Trinity Senator, the classics scholar W.B. Stanford, did not go forward for election. The two other candidates were John Ross (father of Senator Shane Ross) and Mary Bourke.

Of the 6,625 voters in the Dublin University constituency 4,630 voted, giving a quota of 1,158. The result of the first count was:

Skeffington	1,448
Jessop	1,189
BOURKE	1,140
Ross	853

Skeffington and Jessop were declared elected on the first count. John Ross said at that point that he was willing to concede the seat to Mary Bourke but the Returning Officer said the electoral procedure made no provision for that and after the distribution of Skeffington's surplus of 290 votes, 165 went to Mary Bourke and 125 to John Ross giving a second and final count result of:

BOURKE	1,305
Ross	978

Mary T.W. Bourke from Victoria Terrace, Ballina, and Westland Row, Dublin, had entered public life.

At the count centre she gave her first political interview to *The Irish Times*. The Senate, she told the reporter, should be used as a "forum for new and possibly unpopular views". It was the earliest indication of where her political career was heading.

The first commentator to pick up on this potential direction was political writer John Healy. The day after the first meeting of the new Senate, 6 November 1969, he told his readers in *The Irish Times* that Senator Mary Bourke promises to be "the most charming dissenter in the House".

5

THE MOST CHARMING DISSENTER IN THE HOUSE?

The general election campaign of June 1969 made its mark in Irish political history as the one dominated by the most peculiar of native-bred ailments - the "red scare". At the beginning of the year the Labour Party, after sorting out considerable internal wrangling, adopted what was seen during the course of the campaign as a more radical socialist image. That image attained its public manifestation in a phrase from the address by party leader Brendan Corish to the 1967 Party Conference. He told delegates, "The seventies will be Socialist". Mr. Corish told the media that Labour would be the dominant party in the Dublin area after the election. Labour fielded an unprecedented 99 candidates including media personalities like Justin Keating, David Thornley and Conor Cruise O'Brien. Fianna Fáil, then three years under the stewardship of Jack Lynch, went for the Socialist jugular. Party elders like Seán MacEntee (Cruise O'Brien's father-in-law) warned the electorate of "the 'red menace' and the 'red flames' of the burning homesteads of Co. Meath". Michael Moran, the Minister for Justice, spoke of "the new left-wing political queers who have taken over the Labour Party from the steps of Trinity College and Telefís Éireann". To push the point home Jack Lynch beat a path to the well-polished mahogany of convent doors all over the country. The buzz word on the anti-Labour campaign door-steps was "nationalisation." Labour countered with its own smear campaign against the pro-business lobby or "Taca fat cats" in Fianna Fáil. It was all to no avail.

Labour's vote increased in Dublin but plummeted in the country, especially in Munster which had been a Labour stronghold. Overall, the party lost four seats. Fianna Fáil's share of the vote went down but because of successful doctoring of the constituency boundaries by Local Government Minister Kevin Boland, it gained two seats. The final result gave Fianna Fáil 75 seats, Fine Gael 50 seats, Labour 18 and Independents 1. With a working majority of five seats Jack Lynch formed a new government. When the results were declared a political wag remarked, "The Socialists will be seventy."

The new Senate was elected in August 1969. On a quiet news day, the election of a Catholic woman to represent Trinity in the Senate might well be expected to make the front pages. On 13 August the newspaper announcement of Mary Bourke's election to the House was pushed off the front pages by the events that were unfolding in Northern Ireland. The day of the count, two men had been shot in Derry and there were over a hundred casualties after disturbances at the Apprentice Boys parade.

The new senator did make the front pages three months later. One of the first photographs of her as a public figure accompanied a report in *The Irish Times* from John Healy on the election of the chairman of the Senate. The photograph shows her smiling broadly and wearing, at a jaunty angle, a French-style beret. Her mother was of the opinion that some form of headwear was essential for a lady entering public life. Never keen on hats she chose the more casual beret for the occasion. The caption under the photograph no doubt surprised, if indeed it didn't send ripples of shock through her Trinity constituents. It read: "Mary Bourke (F.F.) aged 25, the youngest woman member in the new Senate." Had Miss Bourke joined the Government benches on her first day in the Upper House? She reassured her followers of her independence in a letter to *The Irish Times* which appeared a day after the offending caption:

Sir,
I have no objection, in my capacity as an independent senator representing the constituency of Dublin University, to the (F.F.)

following my name in yesterday's (Nov. 6th) issue, provided this is clearly understood, as I understand it to mean, "friendly face".

Yours etc.,

Mary T.W. Bourke,

Law Library,

Four Courts.

On her first day in the House Senator Bourke came to its attention through an act of dissension. She voted against the election of Michael Butler Yeats as Cathaoirleach (Chairman) of the Senate. It was an interesting scenario. Senator Yeats, a Trinity graduate, became Cathaoirleach of the Seanad with only two dissenting votes ranged against him. Both were Trinity senators - Owen Sheehy Skeffington and Mary T.W. Bourke. Sheehy Skeffington was unhappy with two aspects of Yeats's potential stewardship that rendered him, in his view, unsuitable for the post. There was the matter of his frequently being in a muddle over matters of procedure and, perhaps of more importance to Skeff, as his friends knew him, there was a greater sin. Michael Yeats was a deeply committed Fianna Fáil party man who "never admitted that his party might be wrong", Senator Sheehy Skeffington observed. He had stood in Dublin as a Fianna Fáil candidate in the Dáil elections of 1948 and 1951.

Michael Yeats, whose father, the poet W.B. Yeats, had also been a senator, was popular right across the party divide. When a division was called, Dr. Sheehy Skeffington was left with one lone supporter, the new member for Trinity, Mary Bourke.

In 1969 Mary Bourke was one of the very few women in Irish public life. There were five other women in the Senate but only two in the Dáil. The Civil Service and the professions were still dominated by men. She told the *Irish Independent* soon after her election that she did not believe in "suffragette type activity". She said that for a woman the best way of overcoming prejudice against women is "not to emphasise that you are a woman but to show that you can do a job efficiently and well". Nothing too revolutionary in that safe statement.

41

One of her first public statements on the feminist movement was made in April 1970 in the rather unusual forum provided by a lunchtime lecture at St. Anne's Church in Dublin's Dawson Street. She said she did not support the feminist movements in America because they tended to be extremist movements expressing themselves as a challenge to the social order. "To attain equality," she said, "they adopted a hostile approach to males." Her view was that the true resolution to the lack of equality between men and women was for the two to work together, neither being the tool of the other, with greater options and horizons for women, but at the same time, "Vive la Différence" as she put it.

However, she made it clear from the outset of her public career that she would be especially concerned "both consciously and unconsciously" with matters of particular concern to women.

By 1971, with nearly two years in the Senate behind her, her approach on that same subject was beginning to take on all the appearance of a more radical edge. Speaking to a Christus Rex Congress in Bundoran, Co. Donegal, on the role of women in Irish society, she said that the Women's Liberation Movement constituted the only radical force in the "stagnant pool of Irish life". She condemned Irish legislators for a general lack of initiative in implementing social legislation. When calling for a new vision of Irish society she said, "The only untapped source of new ideas and initiatives left in the country is its women."

Getting to the meat of her address she offered the view that the political awakening of the women of Ireland might be "the lever to break open the rigid structures of the present political parties, which, she told her audience in Bundoran, "had no basis in unity of ideals or viewpoints". Ironically, Mary Bourke was not present when the first major salvo was fired in the battle for that political awakening.

From the viewpoint of historical timing the Bundoran platform may not have been quite the most opportune place for Senator Mary Bourke to be waxing radical. In Dublin's Mansion House at the same time the Irish Women's Liberation Movement was given a major public baptism. In what journalist Elgy Gillespie described as "an atmosphere of charged excitement" a crowd of over a thousand, including some men, filled the assembly room of the Mansion House to hear Nell McCafferty open the meeting.

She declared the aims of the movement to be "one family for one house, equal rights for women in law, equal pay for equal labour and equal educational opportunities". The meeting lasted over three hours. Over 60 speakers addressed the gathering from the floor and at 11 p.m. the queue for the microphone had to be turned away. The youngest speakers were mere teenagers; the oldest was seventy-three-year-old Hilary Boyle. Hundreds of volunteers joined up that evening of 14 April 1971 to form local branches of the movement. The women's movement in Ireland was now well and truly launched.

The Irish Women's Liberation Movement was made up of women who ranged in political outlook from the arch conservative to the bra-burning radical. The debate on women's issues in Ireland began in an atmosphere of amusement and occasional ridicule from sceptical males and not a few sceptical females.

Irish political life in the '60s and '70s did have a place for women. Vast quantities of tea were required to fuel the back-room operations during election campaigns; a token woman became *de rigueur* on most party tickets and the occasional woman made it to the back benches and even some to junior ministerial rank. There it stopped.

In 1968 two women's organisations formed an *ad hoc* committee to investigate the flagrant and embarrassing discrimination against women in Ireland. Their efforts resulted in the establishment of the National Commission on the Status of Women in Ireland on the 31 March 1970. Its brief was to examine and report on the status of women in Irish society. Its findings were to become a *vademecum* for Mary Robinson's public life.

The Commission reported its findings in early 1973. The report looked at several instances of actual discrimination against women and also looked at the broader area of traditional attitudes to women and the stereotyped roles assigned to women in Irish society. The report represented an important first step. The *ad hoc* committee which led to the establishment of the Commission became the Council for the Status of Women.

"The significance of the Irish women's movement," Mary Robinson observed in 1971, "is that it is forward looking and not impressed by Civil War terminology and that it is focused on social injustice."

She had also observed that Irish women had further to come in relation to achievement of equality than any other developed country. A message she repeated regularly at the time exhorted Irish women to be aware that their own potential should lead them to greater participation in the structures and institutions of Irish society.

Article 40 of the Irish Constitution promises equal rights to all of the country's citizens. When Mary Robinson began her Senate career women were treated as second-class citizens. They could not sit on juries, a woman-hour was worth 26p while a man-hour was worth 47p, only six per cent of executive and managerial workers were women, a wife's domicile was wherever her husband chose to live, a woman paying tax on her income forfeited her rebate benefits to her husband, a husband legally received the children's allowance money, his consent was necessary to take the children abroad.

The Married Women's Status Act of 1957 and Ireland's signing of the UN Charter of the Political Rights of Women in 1950 made little practical difference to the way women were treated in Ireland.

Within eight months of her election to the Senate Mary Robinson had publicly criticised the prohibition on divorce under Article 41 of the Constitution and also criticised the prohibition on the sale of contraceptives under the Criminal Justice Amendment Act of 1935. Her view was that Article 41 should not be part of a Constitution but should come under the ordinary process of law. She saw the article as curtailing, not just the freedom of women, but the freedom of the individual. She made her views known to the Alexandra Guild Conference in Dublin in April 1970.

In her paper she was critical of the Constitution's recognition of the special position of the Catholic Church and of other Churches specifically mentioned. She told her audience that it was not sufficient to inscribe rights in a written Constitution; it was equally important, or even more important, she added, to implement those rights.

In one of her first specific references to the prohibition on the sale of contraceptives in Ireland, she said the legislation reflected the views of the Roman Catholic Church. In a democratic society, she told the conference, the law should not be used to uphold or enforce the beliefs of any particular church. In the course of her remarks she praised the work being done by the Fertility Guidance Clinic in Dublin's Merrion Square.

Within six months of her election the young senator had embarked on the sort of liberal crusade that was to set her apart from all but a handful of her fellow senators; put her at odds with the Roman Catholic Hierarchy; alienate her from the mainstream of middle-class Irish life; make her an unpopular figure in the conservative ranks of the Irish Bar and even in the prophet's hometown. The reverse of the medal was that her stand on a variety of issues made her the darling of the growing ranks of Ireland's liberal left and an instant hit as a woman in public life.

Within the same six-month period she openly and regularly voiced the opinion that as a legislator she felt redundant. She told Mary Kenny in an interview in the *Irish Press* that she felt like walking up and down outside the parliament buildings on Kildare Street with a placard which read "I am Under-Employed." She also told Mary Kenny that she found it increasingly difficult to defend parliament against the accusation of her generation that it was becoming irrelevant. She left the readers of the *Irish Press* in no doubt but that it was her view that with just six months behind her in parliament, the institution was, as she saw it from inside, becoming increasingly irrelevant. Her view at the time was that all the important arguments about social and political issues of the day took place outside parliament. Its role, she said, ought to be at the centre of what is going on but instead the institution was becoming an "obsolete, expensive, cumbersome mechanism, purely drafting government legislation".

Throughout her public life as lawyer and senator, Mary Robinson has not been given to colourful excess in her way of speech. Some of her critics saw this as indicating a coldness of personality and a lack of humour. This interview with Mary Kenny in April 1970 is perhaps the nearest she came, with one other exception which we will see later, to what is so often the hallmark of political speeches and interviews in Ireland - an almost theatrical performance played to the gallery. But these were early and inexperienced days for the young senator. She was also discovering, as so many of its members have done before her, that the Upper House is very much the toy of the government of the day.

Despite a certain youthful political naivety, the twenty-five-year-old Trinity senator was learning quickly to use effectively what she had so shrewdly observed about the workings of Irish politics. She too began to make those important statements about social and political issues on a variety of platforms outside the rarefied atmosphere of the Duke of Leinster's former townhouse.

She rounded off her comments to Miss Kenny by telling her that while she was not critical of the Senate's constitutional position, she did feel that it was under-used and acted merely as "a rubber-stamp for the Government". But in that month of April 1970 she was just warming to her theme. In early December, and on the eve of her marriage to Nicholas Robinson, she fired off a salvo in the letters page of *The Irish Times*. "In this time of crisis in our national economy," she wrote, "we cannot afford a Senate which is merely decorative." She pointed out that the House had not met for nearly five months. She softened the line somewhat with a defence of the Second Chamber. "In a democracy," she wrote, "there are sound reasons for retaining a Second Chamber in the legislature, provided it is allowed to play an active role in legislating and debating matters of public interest."

Thomas Garvin in his book, *The Irish Senate*, published the year of Mary Bourke's election to the House, points out that the Senate's uses are potential rather than actual. Eamon de Valera characterised the predecessor of the present assembly as "the vestigial remnant of obsolete constitutional arrangements". Mr. Garvin in his analysis pointed out just what Senator Mary Bourke was discovering for herself the year of her election, when he wrote: "The natural evolution of modern government has made the Executive progressively less prepared to tolerate checks and balances which cannot justify themselves and are more liable to regard interference with its wielding of authority as an attack on its position."

It was just that theme that Senator Bourke had been developing and expanding since she spoke on the subject in the Senate on 2 December 1969. She had on that occasion criticised the tendency of the Government to make policy decisions without reference to specific bodies; to announce them as a *fait accompli* and refer the working out of the policies to the bodies themselves. In the same speech she said the Senate was a place where civil liberties might be discussed and it might have a vital role in anticipating public opinion on the law relating to divorce and contraception. There was, she told the House, "too much double-thinking in this area".

The Report of the Committee on the Constitution was published soon after the senator made those remarks. She became one of the public figures most closely associated with the debate that raged on various constitutional matters throughout the following decade.

Addressing a Civil Liberties forum in Cork in September 1970 she reviewed what she saw as many of the faulty articles in the Constitution. She stressed that what was important was not what was written in the Constitution but how it was applied or upheld by the institutions of the State and by public opinion.

She offered the view that Article 45 was the only Article which was not obligatory in its phrasing but was inserted for the guidance of the Oireachtas. As the Article which dealt broadly with social policy it appealed to her but she said she wanted to see "some teeth put into the Article", so that if the Government was diverted from its course it could still be enforced in the courts.

She told the Cork meeting that "a Constitution should not be fixed;

it should either evolve with the nation itself or else it should be changed from time to time". She concluded by saying that the watchfulness of its people should ensure that the Constitution should mature with the nation.

In July 1970 Senator Bourke accepted an offer from *The Irish Times* to write a "thought piece" on a constitutional solution to the Northern problem. In view of her later resignation from the Labour Party over the Anglo-Irish Agreement, the article is a key document in the canon of her political development.

At its core is the view that Article 3 of the Irish Constitution, which asserts jurisdiction over the whole island of Ireland, puts forward what she called "an unnecessary assertion of jurisdiction" if a functional approach of co-operation with the North and the interdependence of the institutions of the North and the South was to be introduced. She suggested that it should be possible to avoid conceptual notions of sovereignty and to concede the reality of a certain autonomy to the Northern community. Her view was that it would be a consequence of this move that the Northern regime would be less defensive and more prepared to co-operate in the extended structures of the two communities based on the pluralist nature of those communities. Like a scholar or lawyer citing the authority on which an argument or case is to be presented, she told her reader of the grounds or basis for the ideas she was now presenting.

As a Trinity senator, she said, she was accountable to the substantial proportion of her constituency who lived in Northern Ireland. The *Irish Independent* had predicted, just after her election, that her first action as a senator would be to appeal to Trinity graduates North and South to put aside considerations of religion and work together for peace. As an independent senator she said she was in a position to propose a constitutional solution without party political considerations and free of any party whip.

She had urged political parties in the South to establish consensus on a political solution to the Northern problem when the Senate debated a motion outlining the desirability of joint discussion on the

North between the Government and the opposition parties.

In her *Irish Times* article she said that as a Constitutional lawyer and a young person looking to the future of Ireland as a whole she was appalled at the violent and destructive forces within the country which were leading to a polarisation of the Irish people on sectarian grounds. Essentially what the article proposed was an elaboration of a federalist structure with what she saw as sufficient flexibility to make it easier for both communities to focus on constitutional co-operation.

At around the time the article was published, Senator John Horgan, journalist, scholar and Labour Party activist, published the view that constitutional reform might elicit some form of positive response from the people of the North but once that was chosen as the only reason for reform of the Constitution it would cease to have any value with regard to the North at all. He shared with Mary Bourke the view that the most fundamental reason for revising the Constitution would be to give some form of concrete expression to the pluralist society they both believed in.

At the end of 1970, the newly elected senator took a break from the affairs of State. In December 1970 Miss Mary Bourke became Mrs. Mary Robinson. And she would remain Mrs. Mary Robinson, there would be no concession to the feminist Ms.

She married Nicholas Robinson on 12 December at a discreet private ceremony in the chapel of Dublin airport. There was a small gathering of close friends and legal colleagues there to witness the event. Her parents and her brothers did not attend. This was to cause the only major but short-lived rupture in what had, up to this point, been an idyllic family relationship.

Her parents, especially her mother, were conservative Catholics of the old school. In 1970 mixed marriages were still causing problems in many Irish families. There were to be two such marriages in the Bourke family. Mary's brother Oliver later married Louise Perdue, the daughter of the Church of Ireland Bishop of Cork. The family attitude to her marrying a Protestant surprised not only the couple's liberal friends but many in Ballina who recalled that in very recent history the Bourkes, had, after all, been Protestant.

After a champagne reception at the airport Mr. and Mrs. Robinson flew to London before flying to Spain where they honeymooned in Tenerife in a house owned by Nick Robinson's father. Tenerife was still relatively unspoiled by tourism and Howard Robinson's house was an ideal location for a honeymoon, being near the picturesque village of Candelaria and within easy driving distance of Santa Cruz. There they rested and there also Mrs. Robinson could relax before she took on a task with which her name was to become synonymous.

6

A CURSE UPON OUR COUNTRY

⁃ MRS. ROBINSON AND THE CONTRACEPTION CRISIS

During the years that he was Archbishop of Dublin, Dr. John Charles McQuaid was perceived by many within the boundaries of his archdiocese and in far-flung corners of the post Vatican II Church, to be something of an ogre. He was not unaware of this public perception of himself. He sometimes used it to humorous advantage, as at the opening of the Dublin Diocesan Press Office in 1965, when he moved amongst the guests, saying, "So you've come to see the ogre in his den?"

Progressive Church thinkers in Ireland and elsewhere were embarrassed by his resolute and conservative attitude to the changes wrought by the Second Vatican Council. For Dr. McQuaid "nothing had happened in Rome to disturb the tranquillity of Irish Catholic life". "Ecclesia semper reformanda" was not a notion that the Archbishop especially subscribed to, and under his episcopate the reforms set in train by the Council were not embraced too readily in Dublin.

Any Irish politician likely to provoke His Grace's wrath through conflict over legislation had, as a yardstick of its likely effect, the fate of Dr. Noel Browne's Mother and Child Scheme. Due to opposition from the Roman Catholic Hierarchy and conservative elements of the Irish medical profession, amongst other factors, Dr. Browne was unable, as Minister for Health, to introduce the scheme which was provided for under the Health Act of 1947.

Within ten years of her parents seeking his permission for their daughter to enter Trinity College Dublin, Dr. McQuaid would again hear the name of the girl from Ballina in his palace in Drumcondra - in very different circumstances, however. He may well have reflected how wise his counsel would have been had he refused permission for Mary Bourke to be educated at "the Protestant university". The issue which may have prompted such reflection was her desire to change Ireland's law on contraception.

The first legislative initiative to do so came in 1971, not from any Government source but from a number of young senators including Mary Robinson, John Horgan and Trevor West. Their Bill caused Jack Lynch's Government to agree in principle in mid-March to change the law on contraception.

Mary Robinson had chosen the inauspicious date of Friday 13 September 1970 to tell a special meeting of the Medical Union of Ireland that she soon intended to try to have the legislation on contraception amended or replaced.

The theme of that special meeting, attended by nearly 200 of Ireland's leading doctors, was "Family Planning - The Doctor's Dilemma".

The Senator told the meeting that she believed that family planning ought not to be a legal problem. "The law," she said, "has interfered as it should not, in the matter of personal morality. The problem is one for doctors and for personal responsibility." She added, however, that it was a matter where religious counsel could certainly be admitted.

Coming ahead of the storm that was unleashed by Mrs. Robinson's Bill, this Dublin meeting provided her with a valuable insight into the thinking of the Irish medical profession on contraception.

Dr. Derek Waldron-Lynch said he left the meeting with two thoughts in his mind: firstly the necessity and importance of freedom of conscience and secondly, that if that freedom of conscience was to be exercised in Ireland there was a need to change the law on contraception. Dr. Waldron-Lynch's thoughts reflected the mood of the meeting.

Dr. Michael Solomons said that for him the only dilemma in the use of contraceptives would revolve around the best methods for each patient.

The Rev. Denis O'Callaghan, Professor of Moral Theology at St. Patrick's College Maynooth, was pressed by many of the doctors present to give them a simple answer to the question of whether or not it was morally right or wrong for Roman Catholic doctors to prescribe contraceptives for their patients. Understandably, from the viewpoint of a moral theologian no such simple answer was available, but he did see it as a changing situation and he, unlike the hierarchy, did not wish to lay down what sounded like rigid guidelines.

This, of course, was not the position of the hierarchy who were doing just the opposite at this time. Denis O'Callaghan quoted Ian Paisley's famous remark: "For too long the Popish priest has muscled in on the marriage bed." There was, Professor O'Callaghan admitted, "something in that".

Pope Paul VI's 1968 encyclical *Humanae Vitae* made Church teaching on contraception quite clear - artificial forms of birth control were not acceptable. The position under Irish law was not as clear-cut.

The Criminal Law Amendment Act of 1935 prohibited the import of contraceptives for sale; it was less clear on the question of the import of contraceptives for personal use. Under the Act no penalty attached to the import for personal use but, technically, a traveller entering Ireland with contraceptives could have them confiscated but was not, it would seem, liable to any other penalty. A doctor could prescribe contraception but could not fill the prescription except in the case of the pill which was imported into Ireland as a "cycle regulator" and not a contraceptive. In 1971 thousands of women in Ireland were taking the pill for "medical reasons". It should have been obvious to even the most conservative politicians that by 1971 the mood of the country favoured a change in the law on contraception.

At the Fianna Fáil Árd Fheis in 1969, the party leader, Jack Lynch, had said that the question of contraception was a matter of conscience in which the State did not interfere and had no intention of interfering. It seemed a curious statement given that the 1935 Act was still governing the situation with considerable interference. Coming at the time of a proposed change to Article 44 of the Constitution the Taoiseach may have been aiming his remarks North and not South of the border. The remark was also made at a time when Ireland had her sights set on EEC membership. At any rate no change to the law on contraception was made under Mr. Lynch's administration and the Bill introduced by the three senators, which included Mrs. Robinson, did not get a first reading in the lifetime of that Government.

Some members of the Fianna Fáil parliamentary party who were sympathetic to the proposed changes in the law relating to contraception believed the Robinson Bill would cause more delay than was necessary in having the law changed. An unnamed cabinet source told *The Irish Times* that the Bill represented "amateur efforts of some people to get a serious job done in a hurry". In Fianna Fáil cumainn around the country there were many women who favoured a change in the law while most men did not. The situation was similar in most Labour Party branches.

When the proposed Bill was announced Archbishop McQuaid made his position on it quite clear in a letter read at all masses in his diocese on Sunday 28 March 1971. If legislation which offended the objective moral law was passed, he said, it would be "a curse upon our country". The country's Roman Catholic pulpits shook with this warning to the nation's legislators:

"If they who are elected to legislate for our society should unfortunately decide to pass a disastrous measure of legislation that will allow the public promotion of contraception and an access hitherto unlawful, to the means of contraception, they ought to know clearly the meaning of their action, when it is judged by the norms of objective morality, and the certain consequences of such a law."

Echoing the teaching of *Humanae Vitae*, Dr. McQuaid said that contraception was "a right that cannot even exist".

"Government sources" quoted by the *Irish Times* political correspondent, the day after the letter was read, said the Government would "consider the statement" but it was unlikely to delay any changes it proposed to make in the contraception law.

On the same day a doctor working with the Dublin Fertility Guidance Clinic estimated that at least 25,000 women were taking the pill in Ireland. A spokesman for one of the English pharmaceutical companies manufacturing the pill said the numbers using it in Ireland had dropped only slightly after the publication of *Humanae Vitae*.

The Irish Hierarchy was at its most militant on the contraception issue in the period after Mary Robinson's Bill was mooted.

At a confirmation ceremony in Kinsale Co. Cork, the Bishop of Cork and Ross, Dr. Lucey, made it known that "no Catholic can use contraceptives in good faith and with a good conscience except those grossly ignorant or grossly misled".

Another prelate who did not favour a change in the law was the Bishop of Killala, Dr. McDonnell, who resided in Mary Robinson's home town of Ballina. Speaking in St. Muredach's Cathedral, where Senator Robinson's parents attended mass, Bishop McDonnell offered this view to the town's citizens:

"If anyone thinks that the sale of contraceptives might solve some social problems let him think of the dreadful problems it can create. Will this measure," (Senator Robinson's Bill), he thundered rhetorically to his Mayo congregation, "give us a sort of society that we do not want?".

Then he put it to the massgoers in St. Muredach's that they should ponder the question and make their views known to their public representatives, "and not have it appear that the clergy are the only people concerned about this".

Some of the Ballina congregation took Bishop McDonnell's advice and made their views known in the conventional manner; others were more unconventional in their method of communication.

Envelopes with Mayo postmarks arrived on Senator Robinson's desk containing what purported to be used condoms. When actual condoms were not available to the "correspondent" - and if the law was working they should not have been - fingers were cut from rubber gloves as a symbolic alternative.

Quite soon after Mary Robinson became the name most publicly associated with the push to change the law on birth control, abusive letters and phonecalls became a regular feature of her working day.

One Roman Catholic priest who was a friend of her mother's was heard to say in the parish: "Why is Mary doing this to her poor mother?"

Her mother does not appear to have taken her daughter's moves to change the law on contraception in quite the same way as the concerned clergyman. There was certainly no breakdown in communication between mother and daughter over this subject as there had been over Mary's marriage to Nick Robinson. Few worked harder than Tessa Bourke to ensure that once her daughter was elected, she would remain a member of the Irish Senate. In fact, Mrs. Bourke died in Dublin during the 1973 Senate campaign.

As the controversy surrounding the contraception debate intensified, the Roman Catholic Bishops fired off a potent salvo after a special meeting in Maynooth on 11 March. It expressed their "disquiet" on pressures being exerted on public opinion on questions concerning the civil law on divorce, contraception and abortion.

The statement rejected the contention that these three issues were matters of "purely private morality". In one respect the statement amounted to a challenge to the country's politicians when the bishops pronounced that:

"Civil law on these matters should respect the wishes of the people who elected the legislators and the bishops confidently hope that the legislators themselves will respect this important principle."

In the month of March 1971 the bishops felt they had genuine cause for concern. Speaking in the Dáil, just a week before the Maynooth statement was issued, the Foreign Minister, Dr. Patrick Hillery said that "...the good government of Ireland requires us to legislate for the general good, not for our own private satisfaction. The legislature is certainly not bound to express inhibitions in matters in which adult people felt entitled to decide for themselves".

The Taoiseach, Jack Lynch, had said basically the same thing on RTE radio just a month before Dr. Hillery's statement, when he expressed the view that he did not think the State should legislate for private morality.

Fianna Fáil back-benchers came under grassroots pressure to force the Government to drop the issue. The party had no intention of rushing the legislation through parliament.

The statements by Mr. Lynch and Dr. Hillery were intended to be an indication that the Government would not stand fast on the 1935 Act if Senator Robinson's Bill was rejected. Failing to show a willingness to change the law would have upset the scales on which Fianna Fáil's Northern policy was so delicately balanced. It was a matter of credibility, but Fianna Fáil could take comfort from the fact that every party in Leinster House was divided on the issue of contraception.

Fine Gael's cocktail of Catholic constitutionalists, conservatives and a sprinkling of liberals showed no more unity on the issue than was to be found in Fianna Fáil. Most members of the front-bench would not have relished a confrontation with the Hierarchy. In the Senate, Fine Gael's leader in the House, Senator Michael O'Higgins was one of the party's most hard-line opponents of contraception. Orthodox Roman Catholics like Fine Gael TD, Oliver J. Flanagan, were vehemently opposed to a change in the law.

"There is no such thing as a liberal Catholic," Deputy Flanagan told a Fine Gael meeting in Mountmellick, Co. Laois, the month after Mrs. Robinson tried to introduce her Bill in the Senate. He referred to Mrs. Robinson and the others involved in the attempt to change the legislation as "Johnny-come-latelys" in Leinster House who were being used by "outside forces" to undermine Christianity in Ireland. He took comfort from the fact that there were still enough "proud and ignorant" people in Ireland to stand up to them. The people who were now trying to change the law were "not elected by the votes of the people", Mr. Flanagan told his audience and he doubted that they ever would be. "The handful of intellectuals demanding the change," Deputy Flanagan said, "can do untold damage to future generations."

Few Fine Gael deputies were prepared to go on the record in such terms as those used by Oliver J. Flanagan but there were many whose opinion on contraception did not differ greatly from that held by the Laois deputy.

The Labour Party presented a reasonably unified front on the debate, with the exception perhaps of Limerick deputy Stevie Coughlan and one or two others. It stood to gain most at the polls on such liberal issues. Labour, unlike Fianna Fáil and Fine Gael did not depend for its support on the conservative middle ground of rural Ireland. Early on in the debate Labour TD Conor Cruise O'Brien said that if the Government brought in the necessary changes in the contraception legislation it would "be giving the lie in the most clearcut fashion to those who said 'Home Rule is Rome Rule' and that Ireland's legislators were dictated to by the Hierarchy".

Another Labour TD, the Trinity academic David Thornley, said it would be wrong of the Labour Party solely to assume the initiative on the contraceptive issue. He said that to do so would make a political issue of it rather than the moral issue that it was.

While the debate stormed ahead it was joined by the Church of Ireland Archbishop of Dublin, Dr. Alan Buchanan, who said on the RTE current affairs programme *7 Days* that the members of his Church felt they had a right to contraception. The Presbyterian and Methodist Churches were of the same view. The 1971 Spring Synod of the Dublin District of the Methodist Church in Ireland debated the proposed change in the law. It sent the following resolution to the Department of the Taoiseach:

"This Synod believes that liberty of conscience is being infringed by the present laws relating to contraceptive devices and welcomes the Taoiseach's recent undertaking to examine the law where it appears to infringe on liberty of conscience. We think the position is urgent and look forward to early legislation which will give full liberty regarding family planning to all the people of Ireland."

Two Protestant publications carried articles within a month of the proposed changes in the law being mooted by Mrs. Robinson and the Bill's co-sponsors.

"It is a pity," Dean Victor Griffin of St. Patrick's Cathedral Dublin wrote in the Cathedral's monthly bulletin, "that contraception is so often presented as a matter of concession to opinion". He said it should be "treated on a humanitarian and not on a sectarian basis".

An editorial in the *Church of Ireland Gazette* said that the granting of the right of freedom of conscience in a matter that was the private concern of individuals should not have to "wait upon the issue of the theological debate that is taking place in the Catholic Church".

One of the co-sponsors of the contraception Bill, Senator Trevor West, told a meeting of the Literary and Historical Society in University College Dublin that it was "utter nonsense" for a Catholic bishop to say that Protestants in the South were happy with the law on contraception and did not want it. He said the bishops were playing a "political role" in the whole debate.

The public men were having their say in all the usual forums of debate; in parliament, on national radio and television, in the pages of the national and local newspapers, at public meetings, from church pulpits, parish halls and soap-boxes.

But what of the women of Ireland? The Women's Liberation Movement was vocal. Women who were involved with the Fertility Guidance Clinic had their say, housewives wrote letters to the newspapers, some staged demonstrations and walk-outs from churches where they disagreed with the contents of bishops' pastoral letters. The most effective protest in terms of publicity was done in the full glare of the television lights when on 22 May 1971 members of the Irish Women's Liberation Movement brought in contraceptives by train from Northern Ireland in victorious triumph past helpless customs' officials.

The position of the average Irish Catholic mother was rather effectively summed up in a contribution to *The Irish Times* by Mrs. Helen Costello, a Catholic mother of six children, when she wrote:

"You have a two-month-old on one side of the bed, a sixteen-month-old on the other and a two-and-a-half-year-old in another room. Beside you is a husband that you love and who loves you and who has been using his "self-control" for at least four months. So you take a chance and spend the next four weeks (longer if you're breastfeeding) worrying yourself sick wondering whether or not you are pregnant again. This - if you are a practising Catholic - is married life."

"Women like us," she concluded, "wish Mary Robinson luck. There is surely now a majority, if still a very silent one, behind her."

Mary Robinson needed all the luck she could muster to proceed with her plan. She was faced with a Government which paid lip service to changing the law; an opposition which during the early stages of the debate was little better; a Roman Catholic Hierarchy which saw her as the "godless" creature that Oliver J. Flanagan named her as, and finally a Senate which was proving to be the ineffective vehicle she had openly named it to be.

She rose in the rarefied atmosphere of that Upper House under its magnificent stucco ceilings, on 7 July 1971 to attempt to get a first reading for her Bill.

"The reason that Senators Horgan, West and myself tabled this Bill is because we feel that it is a matter of great importance in this country that the law relating to the availability of contraceptives in this country be looked at once again. An obvious way of doing this is to table a Bill to that effect. ...I am disappointed at the reaction of the Leader of the House, who speaks on behalf of the Government on this matter, in view of the many statements made by the Taoiseach and by Deputy Dr. Hillery about the necessity to create a pluralist society in Southern Ireland and the necessity not to discriminate on the basis of religion or on the basis of a majority viewpoint on certain moral questions. I do not know if the Government have changed their minds on this, or whether there has been a change of attitude. If there has been a change of attitude this is very regrettable for those who would like, as I think most senators here would like, to see a better relationship with those living in the North of Ireland. ...If we are serious about the North, we must change our attitudes. We must change our legislation and be able to say to the people in the North of Ireland that they can come into the South of Ireland and find the same tolerance of different moral attitudes, the same tolerance of different ideas, the same possibility of informing themselves on important medical and social matters and the possibility in their own privacy of following their own consciences in relation to family planning."

For the Leader of the House, Tommy Mullins of Fianna Fáil, or Tomás Ó Maoláin as he styled himself in the House, this Bill had become a massive thorn in his side. He became easily irritated when it was raised, accusing its sponsors of disrupting the business of the Senate and accusing Mrs. Robinson of being "schoolgirlish" in her approach. He replied to her on 7 July by saying that the Bill in its present form was unacceptable to the Government and it could not stand over it.

When the question was put, the House divided with the dissenters in the majority. It was clear that the Robinson Bill would face a very uphill battle.

Despite her relentless push to have her Bill accepted, nothing major happened until the slightly more reforming mood of 1974.

In 1935 when the Criminal Law Amendment Act was passed, it met with very little opposition. However, by the time Mary Robinson sought its overhaul the country was in a different mood.

In 1973 Mrs. Robinson came up with a modified version of her 1971 Bill which, unlike its predecessor, was given a first reading. It proposed that the Minister for Health should license the sale of contraceptives through chemists' shops and hospitals. Some contraceptives would be available on prescription only. Its innovative feature was that the Bill would have taken the contraception question out from under the yoke of the criminal law and placed it in the realm of welfare.

She felt confident that neither the legislature nor the Church would block her this time. She told the *Catholic Standard* that while she knew individual churchmen would oppose it she felt "the Hierarchy as a whole would do little to block the new Bill".

This reading of the entrails seemed accurate when on Sunday 26

November 1973 the Roman Catholic Hierarchy published a major statement on its view of Church-State relations. The statement said it was not a matter for the bishops to decide whether the law should be changed or not but it was a matter for the legislature. While the statement reiterated the Church's teaching on contraception as something that was morally wrong, it said it did not follow from that that the State should prohibit the importation and sale of contraceptives. It seemed that the Hierarchy had come a long way from the more intractable position of the late Dr. McQuaid.

John Cooney in his book *The Crozier and the Dáil: Church and State 1922-1986* makes the point that the timing of the bishops' statement was seen by many politicians as unfortunate. "It was issued at a critical juncture," Cooney writes, "when the Sunningdale Agreement was within reach of the formation of a power-sharing executive involving the Ulster Unionists, the Social Democratic and Labour Party and the Alliance Party, and the Dublin Government hoped that this settlement would lead to the setting up of an effective all-Ireland institution."

To Ulster Unionists the bishops' statement might not appear as the old traditional belt of the crozier but rather a new and more subtle form of interference from the Church of Rome. It was significant that Mrs. Robinson and her supporters were not as rattled by the statement as other politicians in Leinster House appeared to be.

That attitude may have had something to do with an impending decision of the Supreme Court which was to give a totally new impetus to the contraception debate. The case was taken by Mrs. Mary McGee, a mother of four children who lived in a mobile home in Skerries, Co. Dublin. Her doctors advised her that she should not have any more children. Mrs. McGee was fitted with a diaphragm, which was to be used in conjunction with a spermicidal jelly with which she was supplied. When her supply ran out she ordered a replacement from England. The package was intercepted by Irish customs officers acting under the 1935 Criminal Law Amendment Act.

Mrs. McGee sought a declaration in the High Court that section 17 of the Act was unconstitutional. Her action failed before Mr.

Justice Ó Caoimh. She appealed her case to the Supreme Court which found that those sections of the Act which forbade citizens to import contraceptives for personal use were unconstitutional. The decision of the Supreme Court was based on the view that family planning rested with the couple alone and that their right to make an unimpeded decision was protected by the Irish Constitution. The *McGee* decision was one of those Constitutional landmarks which most governments fear. It was truly time for the Irish Government to act on the law relating to contraception.

The general election of 1973 had brought Fianna Fáil's 16-year rule to an end. A coalition government of Fine Gael and Labour came to power under the leadership of Liam Cosgrave and Brendan Corish. They had offered the electorate a diet of economic policy and social reform which counter-balanced and outmanoeuvred Fianna Fáil's campaigning on the Northern question. The coalition ruled with a slim majority of two seats. They were now faced with, and embroiled in, the contraception debate.

The debate on the issue opened again in the Senate on 20 February 1974. With over two-thirds of the senators present and the public gallery crowded Mrs. Robinson rose to speak.

She began with a plea to the House that the law of the State should not continue to reflect the morality of one Church but that it should reflect the morality of different outlooks.

She then read into the Senate record, letters expressing the official views of the Church of Ireland, the Presbyterian Church in Ireland, and the Religious Society of Friends, who had written to senators and TDs, untypically, she said, to make their opinions known. She said she hoped the debate would not be treated as a religious one.

In one of the finest speeches of her public career she argued carefully, telling the House that it had two tasks: to regularise the law following the judgment of the Supreme Court in the *McGee* case, and to regularise the law as it stood in relation to family planning and information about contraception.

Ireland, she said, had formally recognised the need for family planning when Resolution No.18 of the UN Conference in Teheran was signed in 1968. She went on:

"We would be hypocrites, we would have no right to the respect of the people in Northern Ireland, we would have no right to self-respect if, having removed the special position of a Church, we continued to embody in our laws the views of a one-denominational outlook which is in conflict with the outlook of the other Churches in this State."

When Mrs. Robinson's Bill reached the second stage in the Senate on 21 February 1974, the coalition decided to act. It did so through the Minister for Justice, Mr. Patrick Cooney, who announced that the Government would publish its own Bill within a fortnight. The Control on Importation, Sale and Manufacture of Contraceptives Bill proposed that contraceptives could be imported and sold under licence by chemists but only to married couples. Mrs. Robinson, whose own Bill suffered defeat in the Senate, said the measure "will to some extent make us the laughing stock of Europe".

It never had the opportunity of achieving that status because in one of the most sensational moments in the voting lobby of Dáil Éireann on 16 July 1974, the Bill was defeated when the Taoiseach, Liam Cosgrave, led six Fine Gael deputies, including Education Minister Dick Burke, sheepishly into the opposition lobby to vote against their own Government's measure. By 75 to 61 votes the Bill was defeated, but the debate was to rattle inexorably on until Charles Haughey, as Minister for Health, offered the Irish nation his "Irish solution for an Irish problem" in 1979.

In the meantime Senator Mrs. Robinson had been busy with other matters.

7

A COMMITTED EUROPEAN

During Mary Robinson's first period as a senator, from 1969 to 1973, it was her involvement in the debate on contraception which captured the headlines. In the background, two other issues, not as controversial as the battle between Church and State over family planning, kept the Senator occupied. While the contraceptive issue gave her much-valued mileage in terms of column inches of publicity, her stand on Ireland's entry into the EEC, and the on-going debate on the Constitution were providing a base from which Mrs. Robinson was building not just her political, but also her legal career.

Mary Robinson was already active on the Executive Committee of the Irish Council of the European Movement when she was appointed, in 1971, to an EEC committee set up to study the extension of the powers of the European Parliament. It was the first time that an EEC body had representatives of applicant countries in its make-up. She was joined by 13 other legal experts who were given six months to examine how the powers of the Parliament might be widened as membership of the Community grew. Her position on the committee gave considerable weight to what she had to say about Ireland's proposed membership of the EEC.

Much of the debate over Ireland's EEC entry was carried on outside Parliament. Mary Robinson regularly raised the subject in the Senate in the course of debates on a wide range of subjects but especially during debates on constitutional questions.

During a debate on EEC membership in the Senate on 11 March 1971 she said she found the three pages of a recent White Paper on membership, which dealt with the constitutional implications, very disappointing. She took issue with the Government over the way it was explaining the membership process to the Irish people and said, during that debate, that joining the EEC "is much more than joining an economic community; it is a fundamental constitutional change". She also urged the setting up of an independent commission on the legal implications of the Common Market.

She told a meeting of Muintir na Tíre in Dalkey, Co. Dublin, in April 1971 that in the event of Ireland's entry into the EEC there would be a contradiction between the requirements of our Constitution and those of the EEC legal system. She must have seen the map of her own future when she told the meeting that it would always be possible for a litigant in an Irish court to appeal to the EEC court even if the decision of an Irish court was upheld by the Constitution.

A referendum on EEC membership was set for 10 May 1972 with Fianna Fáil and Fine Gael supporting membership and the Labour Party and Sinn Féin opposing it. In relation to that referendum Mrs. Robinson told the Senate on 18 November 1971 that she was not satisfied that the constitutional and legal aspects had been properly looked into. It was not easy, she told the House, to have a constitutional change which would achieve the effect of removing inconsistencies in the Irish Constitution. Neither, she continued, was it a matter to be decided in private by an anonymous committee of the Attorney General. She urged consultation with the legal profession.

A week later while addressing the Chamber of Commerce in her native Ballina she expanded on that theme. She described the terms of the Third Amendment of the Constitution Bill as "dangerously wide". The reason for this was that she perceived the proposed change as granting immunity from constitutional challenge to any Irish legislation "consequent on membership of the EEC".

She told her Ballina audience that it was unnecessary to grant such a blank cheque as the Bill offered, as it was dangerous for Ireland's constitutional stability.

She was concerned also that the proposed Bill referred only to the

Community's institutions as they then existed.

Her fear was that as those institutions evolved with the expanding EEC a new Constitutional Bill and a further referendum would be necessary. She said the people should be made aware that a commitment to join the EEC went beyond the Treaties as they then existed. She also said the Government in its approach had opted for pragmatism while she would have preferred honesty and a true commitment to the idea of European integration. In the light of Maastricht her words had a prophetic ring to them.

Back in Dublin in time to address a Christmas luncheon of the Dublin Rotary Club, she spoke on the broader aspects of the European debate.

The country was in danger of being swamped by a tidal wave of "emotional nationalism" she told the meeting in the Intercontinental Hotel.

What was necessary to counterbalance that wave of nineteenth century nationalism, she told her audience, was an examination of the real nature of a European commitment. Social justice could best be obtained in co-operation with partners rather than in competition with other nation states. Ireland's problems could not be seen in isolation from those of the rest of the Continent, she said.

Ireland's application was being debated mostly in terms of economics: the effect on agriculture and industry; higher prices for food; whether the Community's regional policy would benefit us. As a lawyer who had an academic, as well as a practical understanding of the institution, she was one of the few politicians trying to focus in on the broader issues of membership.

At that Dublin meeting she was critical of the undemocratic nature of the Parliament, Council and Commission, remarking how, as then constituted, those institutions were unresponsive to the peoples of the regions.

Early in the New Year of 1972, Senator Robinson sought the support of the Minister for Foreign Affairs, Dr. Patrick Hillery, for reform of the European Parliament. The Community's Committee on the Parliament - the Vedel Committee - on which Mrs. Robinson served, had just reported its findings. It had urged that the Parliament should be given a greater share in decision making, even ahead of direct elections.

Mary Robinson said she thought the best aspect of the Report was that it suggested changes that could be made under the Treaties that were then governing the Community without having to wait for the enlargement of the Community to actually take place. The Senator was only too aware of the Parliament's role as an ineffective talking-shop and she hoped to enlist Dr. Hillery's support to push through the recommendations of the Committee.

Later that year she expressed herself disappointed with the way the Taoiseach, Mr. Lynch, and Dr. Hillery performed at the EEC Summit in Paris on those very points for which she was hoping to enlist their support.

The absence of specific concrete proposals from the Irish representatives to the Summit, she told a meeting of the Irish Council of the European Movement in Dublin, had not helped our image as a small country joining Europe.

It was a scathing attack on the performance of the Taoiseach and Minister for Foreign Affairs at what she saw as an important Summit for a country embarking on Community membership.

She said it was obvious that it was not the Irish delegation which came forward with concrete proposals on regional and social policy. Jack Lynch had returned from Paris in ebullient form. He described the decisions taken as "imaginative and concrete" and he said the main emphasis of the Irish delegation had been on "the urgent need for a comprehensive Community regional policy".

"Is it not astonishing," Senator Robinson asked her audience, "that after months of preparation, after many visits by the Foreign Minister, Paddy Hillery, to Luxembourg, to Rome, to Brussels, that the Irish delegation at the Summit had no specific concrete proposals to make, but just general wishes? We allowed other countries to fight the battle for a specific regional policy and then we came home as though the

68

trophy were truly ours."

She stressed that it would have been more beneficial to Ireland to urge the creation of a real democratic framework at the European level. She said the Summit had been disappointing from the viewpoint of the institutional development of Europe.

The question of the Community's development was confused in Ireland with the question of sovereignty.

She was also concerned at the time that the institutions of the EEC did not facilitate the viewpoint of opposition groups in member states. The institutions of the Community represented the opinion of member governments, she said.

On a number of occasions Mrs. Robinson tried to introduce motions in the Senate relating to the Paris Summit in the hope of having an open debate on the Community's institutional development. Her efforts were of little use.

She raised a number of key questions at that November 1972 meeting. Should the Taoiseach, she asked, have carte blanche to decide Ireland's point of view in the European forum and to take these decisions at the European level? She questioned the weakness of Ireland's democratic institutions which allowed no democratic debate on the issues to be raised at the Summit and she questioned the effectiveness of Opposition views on the same issues.

Always an advocate of strengthening the institutional framework of the Community in a more open, democratic way, Mrs. Robinson was disappointed that the Summit postponed dealing with that question until 1975.

Her address in that Dublin hotel was a warning to the Government and an indication to the 1,041,890 Irish people who voted in favour of joining the EEC that the Senator for Dublin University understood the workings of that institution better than most politicians in the country, and with the alertness with which the *Skibbereen Eagle* had watched Russia, she would be watching developments in the new Europe!

When the magazine *This Week* invited her, in June 1972, to write an article that would consider constitutional issues of interest to her, she wrote that Ireland's entry into Europe "could help to bring North and South closer together". She assumed that, from Brussels, Ireland would be seen as "a geographical unit; a region with similar problems and advantages".

"The concept of quality of life," she wrote, "does not just mean standard of living, it means power to influence decisions affecting the livelihood and environment of the citizen." This was a point she made to the Taoiseach and Minister for Foreign Affairs on their return from the Paris Summit.

Very soon after Ireland's first ten MEPs took their seats in Strasbourg, Robinson continued to push home the point that insufficient attention was being focused on the implications for the Oireachtas of Ireland's membership of the Community.

She held the view that the report of the Vedel Committee, which looked at the Parliament's powers and on which she sat, made it clear that there was insufficient democratic control at European level and thus national parliaments needed to define their roles in the progress towards European integration. In the *This Week* article she argued that centralisation should be combined with devolution to compensate national parliaments for the removal of certain of their decision-making powers.

There was, as Robinson saw it, a two-fold challenge facing the Oireachtas: first, how it should define its role in relation to legislation in the form of regulations and directives coming from the Council and the Commission; second, how the Irish legislature should become aware of and react to policy formation and the EEC's administrative practices. Mrs. Robinson had warned the Government time and again during the debate on EEC membership not to get bogged down on the economic arguments. As someone deeply committed to the European ideal she regularly put forward the notion that what we were joining was not merely an economic community but a "new political and social entity" and Ireland should therefore be ready to take its place as a European state.

8

THE CONSTITUTION AND OTHER MATTERS

Throughout that first period as a senator Mary Robinson led what amounted to a crusade for a secular Constitution. It made her even more unpopular in some political quarters than her attempts to have the law on contraception changed. The old guard in Fianna Fáil saw her pronouncements as aimed at the sacred cow of de Valera's 1937 Constitution and therefore at the old man himself and at the party he founded.

In April 1972 Robinson told a public meeting in Dublin that just as "Irish" and "Catholic" were not synonymous, so "Irish" and "Christian" were not synonymous. Non-Christian Irish men and women, she told the meeting, were entitled to a Constitution to which they could subscribe fully and whole-heartedly. This did not mean that the Constitution would not protect religion; it did so in guaranteeing freedom of conscience and belief.

While she was embroiled at all, she decided to go the whole hog, in remarks guaranteed to annoy the majority of the country. She suggested that the phrases "In the name of the Most Holy Trinity" and acknowledging our obligations to "Our Divine Lord Jesus Christ" should be removed from the Constitution because they were "divisive" and "superfluous". The words "under God" in Article 6, which states that "all powers of government, legislative, executive and judicial, derive under God from the people" should also be scrapped, she said.

She also referred to an oath she later took herself, that of the President, who swears on taking office, "In the presence of Almighty God..." This excluded some citizens from taking it, she said, and there ought to be provision for "the taking of a solemn affirmation instead of an oath, as there is in a court of law."

She called on all politicians in the Republic to make the case for a secular Constitution. Such a Constitution would be a unifying and strengthening force because all Irish citizens could adhere to it with equal loyalty and fidelity.

Coming from Mary Robinson, a lawyer and Trinity academic, such calls were viewed as statements of historical orthodoxy rather than effective political clarion calls.

In his *States of Ireland*, Conor Cruise O'Brien has observed how in Ireland "the affairs of the new State were not long administered in a purely secular spirit". It was this very situation that the Trinity Senator was now addressing.

Speaking at a meeting of the Dublin branch of Tuairim on the subject "Republic of Ireland: a Catholic State for a Catholic People" she said that a Catholic State was no more desirable than a Communist State, because it meant that certain citizens who were of a different religion or no religion could feel that the laws discriminated against them. A Catholic State was less desirable than a State which allowed the maximum freedom of action consonant with public order and security.

In some respects, she said, the Republic was open to this criticism. Statistically, she added, Ireland had a pluralist society but legally that was not the case.

On 1 September 1972 she launched a "campaign" for a non-denominational state. It followed the SDLP's call for revision of the 1937 Constitution along the lines she favoured. A letter from Senator Robinson and Dublin solicitor John Temple Lang appealing for a non-denominational State, appeared in *The Irish Times*:

"We invite everyone who is concerned about the Northern situation, and in particular everyone who saw the need to take an active part in the discussion about the EEC entry, to join us in insisting on this. It is in the economic, social, cultural, and political interests of industry, labour, farmers, hoteliers and the whole Irish community to

72

demand a referendum on these lines. It is also the right thing for them to do for the Republic and for the North. Because it would totally alter the atmosphere in the North, it is a prerequisite for any other constructive action by anyone in the Republic. We invite all sectors of Irish society to recognise their interests and their opportunity, and to launch a campaign on the scale and with the energy which was applied to the EEC question."

In her article in *This Week* (referred to above) she put basically the same view:

"The 1937 Constitution is one of the few in the world which contains an absolute prohibition on granting divorce, reflecting the teaching of the Roman Catholic Church as a constitutional principle. We have a pluralist society in the South for which this Constitution is inadequate. It would not be enough to adopt a blandly Christian Constitution, eliminating the exclusively Roman Catholic provisions. We must be prepared to separate Church and State in the full sense and enact a secular Constitution to which all citizens can adhere equally."

It would be nearly ten years before another such constitutional "crusade" would be launched and in that time not much would have changed. Garret FitzGerald would launch his own "crusade" to persuade the people of Ireland "to adopt the principles of Tone and Davis" - principles, he said, Fianna Fáil did not believe in. The difference was, of course, Dr. FitzGerald was Taoiseach, Mrs. Robinson a non-party, university senator. Before her first period in the Senate drew to a close she concentrated on a handful of other issues.

Supported by Senators Evelyn Owens and John Horgan, Mary Robinson introduced the Adoption Bill (1971) which was an attempt to reform the existing legislation which had been on the statute books for over 20 years with only one minor amendment made in 1964.

There was widespread dissatisfaction among adoptive parents and social workers and others working in the area of adoption. Mrs. Robinson was keen that Section 12 of the 1952 Act under which parties to a "mixed" marriage could not adopt, should be changed.

She succeeded in getting the Bill to a second reading in the Senate and that was a major achievement. The Government promised to introduce its own legislation but the proposers did have the benefit of a full-scale debate in the House in July 1972.

The following November, Fianna Fáil introduced a controversial anti-IRA measure, the Offences against the State (Amendment) Act. The nature of the legislation gave rise to widespread criticism. It had very broad terms, including a provision which said the word of a Garda Superintendent was enough to support evidence of IRA membership. Fine Gael, with some exceptions, and Labour had decided to oppose the Bill but on the day of its second reading in the Dáil two bombs exploded in Dublin. Two men were killed and 127 people injured. It dramatically altered the course of the Dáil crisis over the Bill. It passed all stages by 69 votes to 22 at 4 a.m. on the morning of 2 December.

Senators were summoned by telegram to a 3 o'clock sitting of the House the following day.

Mary Robinson was unhappy that the measure had not received proper consideration in the Dáil and Senate so she tried to introduce an amendment. The idea behind the move was to have it declared emergency legislation under Article 24 of the Constitution. That would have had the effect of keeping the measure on the books for a period of only 90 days unless renewed by either House of the Oireachtas. The attempt to introduce the amendment failed and Mrs. Robinson was of the opinion that another piece of legislation was on the statute books which curtailed the liberty of the individual in the South.

In the dying moments of the life of that Senate, Mrs. Robinson returned to one of her favourite themes.

"Make no mistake about it," she told the Senate, "this House is not in the mainstream of Irish life at the moment. It is not fulfilling a role leading to the exercise of democratic control over Government activity or participation in the legislative process. It is time to say that the Oireachtas is fast rendering itself redundant..."

She was critical of the Senate because it was failing to exert any real influence on the political life of Ireland. She was one of the few senators on record as saying that the House did not meet often enough, nor probe deeply enough into the legislation which came before it. Few senators knew more than she how any form of legislative initiative was discouraged outside the ranks of Government. The Report of the Inter-Party Committee on Dáil Reform which had suggested only minor procedural reforms had been a major disappointment to her. The European parliamentary model is what she advocated at this time, especially its committee system, which she favoured. She was to return to that theme again and again in the course of her Senate career.

Almost four years after she had offered herself to the electors of Dublin University, as an unknown quantity, it was now time for her to make up her mind whether or not she wished to continue to be part of a political system of which she was so highly critical.

There seemed to be not as much need for oracle consulting as there had been in 1969 and she decided to offer herself again and to seek, according to her manifesto, a mandate based "not on promise but on performance".

In that 1973 manifesto she wrote that she offered herself for re-election with even more enthusiasm and a deeper sense of purpose. In a tightly worded, cleverly constructed document, she told the voters of her first term as senator; and of her legislative record. She outlined matters of particular concern to Trinity and finally she wrote of the challenge which lay ahead. That challenge centred mostly on Ireland's EEC membership.

She concluded with an appeal to the voters:

"There is much unfinished business. It has been important to learn the intricacies of parliamentary procedure in order to influence policy and initiate reforms. My appeal is to the young and to the older generations who are young at heart. If re-elected I undertake to apply myself with energy and enthusiasm to the tasks ahead. I ask for a mandate to continue."

The voters were reminded that it would take over 1,300 votes to get her elected and that there was no room for complacency; every vote, especially the first preference vote, was vital if she was to be returned to the Senate.

9

RETURN OF THE DISSENTER

After four years of exposure to the cut and thrust of public life in Leinster House Mary Robinson was in a better position to know the mechanics of getting elected than she had been on her first electoral outing.

The base of operations was moved from 21 Westland Row to her new family home 17 Wellington Place.

What had not changed for this second campaign was the key personnel. Trevor West, her first election agent, was now a candidate himself. He was replaced by J.S.R. Cole, the Senior Lecturer in Law at Trinity.

Tessa Bourke came up from Ballina to cook meals and give moral support. Adrian Bourke gathered the usual team and co-ordinated the media coverage and rattled his friends for support for his sister. Legions of envelope stuffers were guided in their task by Ann Lane. Former classmates and Trinity friends were called on to write letters of support - "topping and tailing" as it was called.

A campaign worker remembers that particular campaign as being a good humoured affair and fun to work on, perhaps, she said wryly, because there seemed to be "endless quantities of litre flasks of Paul Masson wine, provided by Ann Lane, to stoke the engines".

The candidate was proposed, as last time out, by the head of the Law School at Trinity, Professor C.B. McKenna and seconded by her father-in-law Howard Robinson. Many of the names that had lent their support in 1969 appeared again on the 1973 manifesto with the addition of many more.

This time out the Dublin University seats were contested by a much larger field than Mary Robinson faced in 1969. Ten candidates offered themselves for election.

Among them was Dr. Noel Browne, the former Minister and Labour TD for Dublin South East in the outgoing Dáil. He had refused to endorse the coalition agreement between his party and Fine Gael and had not sought re-election to the Dáil.

Dr. Browne's election agent was Dr. David Thornley, ever the Labour Party maverick, who explained his support for Dr. Browne in a press statement:

"No matter what political differences may exist between Dr. Browne and myself, I feel that upon his record of political integrity and service to the nation, particularly as Minister for Health, his removal from public life would be a tragic loss. As a Fellow of TCD I feel entitled to support any other graduate as a Senate candidate..."

The other candidates were: Mary Robinson; Dr. David Cabot, a scientist with An Foras Forbartha (the National Development Agency); Lionel Flemming, a staff journalist with *The Irish Times*; Nessa O'Byrne Healy, an auctioneer; Professor W.J.E. Jessop, an outgoing senator; Dr. Derek Waldron-Lynch, a medical doctor; Joe Revington, who then worked in his family's business in Tralee Co. Kerry; Dr. Trevor West, a mathematics lecturer in TCD and an outgoing senator who won the seat in the Senate by-election which occurred after the death of Senator Owen Sheehy Skeffington; and Dr. David McConnell, a genetics lecturer at Trinity.

When the votes were counted in Trinity's Public Theatre on Tuesday 2 May 1973, Mary Robinson had advanced from a situation which had seen her as last candidate elected in 1969 to now heading the poll.

She polled 1,472 first preference votes. The quota was 1,213. Trevor West took the third seat, defeating W.J.E. Jessop in the sixth and final count. Noel Browne polled 944 first preference votes and was elected on the fifth count. His election was not in doubt as he consistently polled a greater number of transfers than the other

78

candidates.

In the overall situation in the Senate the new Coalition gained control. Fianna Fáil losses included the outgoing Cathaoirleach Michael Cranitch, Neville Keery and Peggy Farrell. Coalition senators were in the majority on the Cultural and Educational, Agricultural and Labour Panels which provide more than half the members of the House. It may have looked, even to Mary Robinson, that the Senate in which she was about to take her seat had a somewhat more liberal make-up than the Senate she had just left behind.

10

THE HAND THAT ROCKED THE CRADLE

"Those who know her well, let it be said, appear to be under oath, to reveal nothing about her; if she is reticent about her professional achievements, she is Sphinx-like about her personal life."

Friends old and new agree with that assessment of Mrs. Robinson by *Irish Times* journalist Mary Maher. They also agree that her election to the Presidency has not altered that Sphinx-like reticence about her family life. Now she has the added paraphernalia of a Constitution, a Civil Service infrastructure and a Special Adviser to stand sentinel to the private and the public life.

For the 20 years that she sat in the Senate, Mary Robinson was rarely out of the public eye, but throughout that period there were few politicians more resolute than she about keeping family and public life in very separate compartments.

No colour features on "The Robinsons at Home" appeared in the national press until the presidential election campaign of 1990. Nick Robinson, through his work for such organisations as the Irish Architectural Archive and in his role as a collector, was sometimes featured in the glossy magazines.

When their first child Lucy Terese, called Tessa, was born on 2 October 1972, Mary and Nick Robinson declined to talk to the newspapers saying they wanted to keep the matter "as private as possible".

This refusal to allow the public "camera-eye" to look at the family in its lair and provide, perhaps, a softening touch, contributed to Mary Robinson's public image as a hard-edged, tough professional woman.

A profile of Mary Robinson in *Hibernia* in 1978 cast her in the role of a "Joan of Arc of the trendy left". The profile appeared under a "Littleman" cartoon of her as a voluptuous Joan about to be torched at the stake until rescued by a smiling Nick Robinson, who is cast, not as a knight in shining armour, but a knight in Harris tweed!

In that *Hibernia* profile Jim Corrigan caught something of the essential Robinson when he described her on a public platform speaking on one of her pet subjects - the rescue of Wood Quay from the planners:

"...Her departing declamation to the marchers, 'I salute you', had something of a faintly Gaulist ring about it, reminiscent of the General's notorious 'I understand you' to his Algerian supporters."

Corrigan saw her, as did other political commentators who profiled her in the '70s as being "as hard-necked a politician as any Fianna Fáil grassroots operator". As if to take the sting out of some of his remarks in the profile, he added: "She is bound to go far in her chosen profession, whatever and wherever this turns out to be".

She was deeply hurt, a friend recalls, when *Hibernia* described her as totally devoid of humour. It was more often her colleagues at the Bar who referred to her lack of humour. She did not partake of those now legendary boozy lunches for which the Bar was justly famous in the 1970s. She also had a reputation of looking somewhat disdainfully on those barristers who plied their trade, for ready money, in the Round Hall of the Four Courts.

The type of legal work she engaged in did not present too many occasions for Wildean wit and her public speeches were usually too weighty for the insertion of a well-prepared joke.

Family and very close friends, like her private secretary Ann Lane, are quick to dismiss the charge that she is humourless and stiff. Ann Lane says Mary Robinson has always had a capacity to laugh at herself.

Mary Robinson tells the story of being in Japan with Nick Robinson when all the Japanese officials thought the tall bearded man was the senator. There has been no such confusion abroad in recent times. When she was told that the Irish Wax Museum was making a model of her for its collection she asked if it was going to be mechanical. This would be necessary, she said, because the head would need to nod up and down if it was to be an accurate image of her!

When covering the President's first official visit to the United States in October 1991 for RTE News, I had occasion to develop a ploy to get access to the Presidential party, often through an off-putting cordon of very heavy-handed Secret Service agents. When we arrived at a new venue, Tim Ryan of the *Irish Press* and myself would address one another in loud voices as "Ambassador". This had the desired effect and the sea of Secret Service agents would part to let us through. When I arrived to interview her for the *Nine O'Clock News* in her hotel suite in Boston she greeted me with "Good evening, Ambassador" - much to my surprise and that of Dermot Gallagher, Ireland's Ambassador to Washington, who was also in the room!

She is not easily thrown by potentially awkward and embarrassing public incidents. RTE's Health Correspondent, George Devlin, recalls that when she visited an old folks home in Dublin one old lady took a particular shine to her and engaged her in a long conversation. When she made to leave the old girl thanked her with the words, "Bless you for coming to see us, Mrs. Thatcher!" The recently elected President didn't bat an eyelid.

The Robinsons have only moved their family home twice in their married life. The first move was the rather short distance from Wellington Place in Dublin 4 to Sandford Road in Dublin 6. The second move was to Áras an Uachtaráin in Phoenix Park.

Number 17 Wellington Place was purchased from Nick Robinson's brother, Peter. His father, Howard, was living in the mews house at the rear of the property. Nanny Coyne came to look after the whole family. Number 17 was a Regency house with three reception rooms, three bedrooms and a good sized garden.

Number 43 Sandford Road was a more spacious house which allowed the senator to have her office in her home. This was done with a view to spending more time with her children. By 1982, when the Robinsons had purchased the Sandford Road house at auction for

£185,000, the family had increased. A son, William, was born on 11 January 1974, and another son, Aubrey, was born on 3 May 1981. The family moved in and Ann Lane set up the senator's new base of operations.

Mary Robinson got the rough edge of some women's libbers tongues for her decision to marry and start a family almost immediately after marrying. She went on record as saying she always wanted children and never considered putting it off so that she could advance her career.

"I had a terribly happy childhood and I have always had this sense of a happy family and wanted children immediately," she told journalist Christina Murphy.

The more radical feminists who embraced her as their champion on liberal issues did not welcome her telling the newspapers that she never once thought of postponing marriage for her career. She told Christina Murphy that she very much wanted to marry Nick Robinson and that she found marriage an "extremely liberating experience". Marriage gave her a "greater sense of confidence and stability", she said.

Christina Murphy remembers asking her why she changed her name so readily, when she was established and well-known as Senator Mary Bourke. She told Miss Murphy that she changed her name to Robinson because she wanted to make a deliberate commitment to Nick. Some people, especially political reporters, found it difficult to get used to her as Mrs. Robinson. She is a woman who, as Christina Murphy observed, has been famous under two names.

The most surprising part of what is perhaps the most open interview she ever gave - certainly on personal matters - is when she said to Miss Murphy that both in politics and law she found that she could do many things more easily as a married woman.

"I found my liberation in marriage," she said in that 1977 interview. The sort of things she was saying to Christina Murphy all indicate that the view of her that was prevalent in Ireland as the hardened, self-seeking feminist, was somewhat wide of the mark. Of motherhood she said: "The children are a great reserve of strength for me; when I'm feeling depressed, they can lift me like nothing else."

"I must be a very difficult person to be married to," she confessed to Christina Murphy, "but I'm extremely lucky to be married to somebody who is not at all put out by my numerous activities."

Mary Robinson has said very little in interviews about her relationship with her husband. "I'd love to be able to say that Nick was great at changing nappies and so on... but he's not. But then I started off as a novice, too, and we just muddle along together," she told Christina Murphy.

Close friends say Nick Robinson is more outgoing than his wife and tends to do more of the talking at dinner parties. For their two family homes he made all the decisions regarding the furnishings and paintings. Mary Robinson had very little input into the decoration of either house. He usually bought period furnishings in places like Dublin's Francis Street or bought from their Sandford Road neighbour, antiques' dealer Val Dillon. Decorative rugs came from Empires in the Westbury Mall. The overall effect was more comfortable than grand. Next door to the Robinsons in the Dillons' property there is one of the finest town gardens in Europe. Spurred on by the Dillons, Nick and Mary Robinson made an occasional stab at doing their own garden but invariably such efforts were abandoned in favour of family, books and work.

Her sense of family has always been of the utmost importance to Mary Robinson. She was conscious of the sacrifice her mother made in abandoning her medical career to bring up her young family. She has made a point throughout her working life of making breakfast for the family whenever time allows. She still does that today. She has referred many times to just how lucky she considers herself, to have been part of two happy families. She has also said how aware she has been through her years in politics of the fact that there are many unhappy families in Ireland into which partners are locked through the constitutional prohibition on divorce.

She criticised the constitutional ban on divorce as early as April

1970, saying that Article 41 of the Constitution, which forbids divorce, "curtails the freedom of the individual". She was in favour of calling a referendum (long before it happened in 1986) to end the constitutional ban on divorce.

Mary Robinson made a decision in 1969 to enter politics on the issues which concerned her most: civil liberties, human rights and family law. By the time Jack Lynch had called a snap general election in February 1973 she was a household name as champion of those sometimes thorny liberal issues and she was once again in parliament representing Trinity College and now a somewhat larger constituency of Irish liberals.

11

CONFUSED LIBERAL?

On Saturday 26 October 1974 Dr. Conor Cruise O'Brien, Minister for Posts and Telegraphs, was guest speaker at the annual dinner of St. Andrew's College Union in Dublin.

In the course of his after-dinner address the Minister turned his attention to a recent meeting which had been organised in Dublin by the editor of *Hibernia*, John Mulcahy. It had, as its theme, internment without trial in Northern Ireland.

Dr. O'Brien accused Mary Robinson of having taken part in a meeting which he saw as "so profoundly illiberal as actually to cast scorn... on the central institution of democracy, parliament itself." The speakers at that meeting in Dublin's Mansion House included the Dungannon priest, Dr. Denis Faul; the editor of *Hibernia*, John Mulcahy; the Queen's University Belfast academic Tom Hadden; the actress Siobhán McKenna and Paddy Joe McClean, who had been interned three times.

The atmosphere of the meeting was described by Eileen O'Brien in *The Irish Times* as one which "degenerated into a shouting match" as Provisional (IRA) supporters prevented speakers from being heard. Mary Robinson told the meeting she saw internment as something which "transgresses the whole principle of law and is contrary to the most fundamental function of the process of law".

"The greatest tragedy in Northern Ireland," she said, "is that a section of the population regard the law as a tyranny, a brutality, that discriminates against them in an arbitrary and unjust fashion."

It had surprised her that the legal profession had not been in the vanguard in protesting against what she called "the tyranny of internment". It was a reflection on the legal profession and the judiciary, she told the crowded meeting, that they could operate side by side with internment. It was one of the strongest attacks she was ever to make on her own profession. It must be said, however, that it was made at a meeting where strong attacks and strong opinions were the flavour of the evening.

The mood of the meeting can be gauged by the reaction to Fr. Denis Faul when he denounced what he called "the IRA murder gangs". The hall resounded to stamping, booing and shouting. Men rose to their feet to denounce the Dungannon priest.

When Tom Hadden suggested that the anti-internment campaign should be detached from the Republican movement, he too was shouted down. He was lucky to escape a lynching when he suggested that trial without jury should continue but that assessors should sit with the judges.

Mrs. Robinson got an easier passage when she said it would be a pity if the impression were created that those against internment were those active in Republican politics. She denounced internment as something "which must be condemned by every citizen who has any respect for the institutions and laws of the State".

In the autumn of 1974 the flagship of RTE's current affairs programmes, *Seven Days*, did a two-part programme on the internment issue. The programme was regarded by the Coalition Government as a highly emotional view of the subject. In part two of the programme, John Kelly, the Government Chief Whip, appeared to be defending the principle of internment.

The strain caused by the internment debate in the relationship between RTE and the Government was correctly gauged by Donal Foley in *The Irish Times*. "Politically," he wrote, "the whole situation regarding the political coverage by RTE could well be the most explosive issue in the Dáil. Fianna Fáil is placed in an invidious position. Mr. Gerry Collins the previous Minister (for Posts and Telegraphs), was looked on by most RTE people as repressive. They now regard Dr. O'Brien in the same category."

The 1974 Labour Party Conference was memorable for a number of reasons. One of the more colourful events for which that gathering has earned a place in Irish political history is known as "the finger wagging episode". It was reported at the time that a group of journalists witnessed the Minister with responsibility for RTE, Dr.O'Brien, wagging his finger at the station's Head of Current Affairs, Desmond Fisher, in admonishment for the *Seven Days* programme on internment. The Minister was alleged to have told Mr. Fisher that the programme was the last exercise of that type that he would be allowed to make. Ministers of the Coalition Government were often seen as favouring a tough line on law and order. Dr. O'Brien was the Cabinet Minister most frequently cast in that role.

When he turned to the meat of his address on internment at the St. Andrew's Union dinner, Dr. O'Brien said that the *Hibernia* meeting on internment, which Mrs. Robinson had addressed in the Mansion House, was "a classic illustration of the confused and confusing alliance between militarist Republicans and a certain kind of Irish liberal".

There was one incident at the meeting which particularly annoyed the Minister. Seán Keenan, a well-known Republican figure from Derry, had called for a picket to be placed on every British establishment in Dublin, the chief of which he considered to be the seat of the Irish Parliament, Leinster House.

That incident became the focus of an attack which Dr. O'Brien directed at Mary Robinson. She had been pilloried by back-benchers and county councillors of all parties for her Contraception Bill; she received more hate mail than any politician or public figure in the Republic; she was now being attacked by a minister - whose party she was soon to join - as someone who failed to defend the honour of the parliament in which she had a seat.

"A member of our parliament," Dr. O'Brien told the Old Boys of St. Andrews "sat on that platform while Mr. Seán Keenan was applauded for describing that parliament as a British institution. She

89

appears to have made no public protest at this proceeding, although she continues to hold her seat in the institution thus held up to contumely."

Dr. O'Brien's view of the meeting was that it was so profoundly illiberal as to cast scorn, not on any political party or the Government itself, but on parliament, the central institution of democracy. Dr. O'Brien was also unhappy with Mrs. Robinson's views on internment as expressed at the meeting:

"The Senator, who is also a Professor of Law, ably attacked the practice of internment without trial, and made the case for reliance on the ordinary courts. But she is not recorded in any reports that I have seen as referring at all to the difficulties which can be experienced under certain conditions in the courts of dealing with armed conspiracies."

This "confused liberal" view of Senator Robinson was not one she took lightly. In fact, in that October twilight the gloves were off and battle ensued between two of the intellectual Titans of modern Irish political life.

Robinson told the *Sunday Press* that Dr. O'Brien was capable of "a personal vendetta" and that he was well known for his animosity to *Hibernia* and spoke of 'Hibernia liberals'.

When she spoke on the RTE programme *This Week* she had softened the tone of her remarks somewhat. She told the interviewer, Seán Duignan (now Government Press Secretary), that the Minister's view of the meeting in the Mansion House was the mistaken impression of one who was not there. She chose to dismiss the description of Leinster House as part of the British establishment as an "old hoary chestnut" that she could spend her time refuting at student debates. Dr. O'Brien, she declared, had used the weight of his office, and the guaranteed publicity, to smear the liberal voice. In a clear reference to an issue with which Dr. O'Brien was closely associated in the public mind, she announced her intention to put down a motion in the Senate on Section 31 of the Broadcasting Act. The Section - the subject of a recent successful legal challenge - effectively muzzled RTE's capacity

90

to interview members of Sinn Féin. Attempts by the Coalition Government at what she saw as unnecessary censorship gave her cause for grave concern. "At this time in Ireland," she told Seán Duignan, "there might be an attempt to squeeze out the liberal voice, stifle it, contain it, or stereotype it."

Mrs. Robinson objected in the interview to Dr. O'Brien's reference to the "confused and confusing alliance between militarist Republicans and a certain kind of Irish liberal". She said she appeared on the *Hibernia* platform as an independent senator and a professor of law and she reserved the right to speak, condemning the principle of internment without trial.

When asked if she accepted Dr. O'Brien's view that Irish liberals could, without knowing it, be helping the IRA she replied:

"It is disquieting that the Minister should express this viewpoint as a Minister. I am not saying that Dr. O'Brien is not entitled to criticise - he is particularly entitled to criticise me because he is a constituent of Dublin University - but he was using the weight of his office... to smear the liberal voice as having been in deliberate alliance, or, worse still, confused alliance with activists. There is great danger in that. We need a strong liberal voice and more parliamentary control, in the true sense, over the activities of Irish life."

The interview concluded with a refutation of the most serious and potentially damaging remark of Dr. O'Brien's, namely that she had not condemned the killing of judges. Her refutation is work quoting in full:

"That is a very slanted point of view. Does he really think that I condone the killing of those judges? He said I attacked the integrity of those judges. In fact, I condemned the silence of the legal profession, including the judiciary, at the operation of internment. They operate side by side with a system which undermines the legal process and is a fatal flaw in bringing up society, creating confidence and building, in an alienated minority, trust and faith in the system."

If this whole debate with Dr. O'Brien served any useful function, it is the understanding it has given us of just exactly which liberal mould Mrs. Robinson saw herself cast from. The two protagonists were given an opportunity to debate their differences of opinion, arising from the controversial internment meeting, when they came face to face on RTE's radio programme *Here and Now*. The programme devoted half an hour to their opposing definitions of liberalism.

Dr. O'Brien offered the view that liberals should be conscious of and seek to avert threats to freedom from any corner. Those threats could come from the State, political parties and from organised groups in society. He said that Senator Robinson's kind of liberalism was useful but it was too narrowly concentrated in one direction. But what was her definition of liberalism?

"Liberalism is the voice of dissent," she said, "especially when that entailed essential human rights."

She quoted Woodrow Wilson's famous remark that the history of liberty was the history of resistance. More significantly she defined the liberal voice as "essentially one which must prevent the encroachment of Government power... and prevent the corners being cut at a difficult time".

The senator said that at that time people were afraid to speak out on issues which needed to be publicly discussed. How was this debate which followed the row with Dr. O'Brien likely to affect her capacity to speak out?

"There is a danger from now on," she told her radio audience, "I will have to exercise a self-censorship. Am I going to have to watch myself? I accept that a liberal can be a dupe. The freedom to choose the platforms on which I speak is something I will have to watch carefully."

One platform on which she delivered some of her most striking public speeches was provided by the campaign to save the Viking settlement found at Dublin's Wood Quay. In the course of salvage excavation work at the site of a new municipal office complex, archaeologists discovered some of the most significant Viking finds ever made in Europe. If they could have been preserved on site they would have provided what one expert called a "veritable map of the medieval town". The impetus to save the site from the developers' bulldozers rested not with Ireland's National Museum but with an *ad hoc* group of writers, teachers, lawyers, political figures and thousands of ordinary Dublin citizens. Their combined efforts kept the bulldozers at bay for over eight years.

Mary Robinson offered her skills as politician and as lawyer, speaking on the subject in the Senate and representing Rev. Professor F.X. Martin in his High Court battles with the developers.

In *Wood Quay: The Clash Over Dublin's Viking Past*, Thomas Farel Heffernan draws this portrait of Mary Robinson as Wood Quay campaigner:

"She has great presence before audiences. Her public voice, in fact, is often so grave and magisterial that it seems to be coming from someone other than the pretty young woman in the front of the room. Her private conversation is warm and enjoyably seasoned with irony."

Mary Robinson's prominence on the Wood Quay platform played no small part in securing her election to Dublin City Council, as indeed the absence from that very platform played no less a part in the failure of people like Dublin's Lord Mayor, Paddy Belton, to be returned to the Council. "I have been ruined by women and by Wood Quay," the defeated Lord Mayor was heard to say.

Wood Quay was of course a national issue. Mary Robinson had a penchant for national issues but it was local issues which preoccupied the voters, as she discovered when she faced into her first attempt to secure a seat in Dáil Éireann.

12

RATHMINES WEST

- EGYPT IS BACKING MRS. ROBINSON

In the public perception Mary Robinson has been inextricably associated with the Irish Labour Party and the Irish Left. In fact, hers was a late vocation. In the 20 years that she was in politics, she spent only nine of them as a member of the Labour Party. She explained her reluctance to commit herself to a political party as having a great deal to do with her commitment to the role of an Independent in Irish politics who took time to adjust to the idea of being a team member. "I suppose I could have joined Labour sooner," she said in 1976, "I was ready to; but I hadn't quite made the psychological break."

When she had made that necessary break she put her reasons for joining Labour on paper, in a letter to *Hibernia* in April 1977:

"The reason I joined the Labour Party is because I am committed to a socialist and democratic state, with radical changes to our structures, in control of wealth and power and in equality in its real sense rather than just paper equality."

Her letter of application to the Party had all the intensity of a manifesto:

"We need a vision of Irish society which is sensitive to the needs and aspirations of all our citizens, and which provides a coherent framework based on fairness, equality of opportunity and social justice. I believe that the Labour Party is the political party which has the potential to build such a society, based not on ideological clichés, but on a flexible and imaginative adaptation of the principles of socialism and democracy..."

The timing of Mrs. Robinson's first attempt to join the Labour Party was unfortunate. It coincided with the Coalition Government's decision to introduce the Emergency Powers Bill - a measure whose passage through parliament she strongly resisted.

To avoid risking an immediate confrontation with the Government in the Senate she delayed her application for Parliamentary Party membership. The move outraged some of the party elders who expected her to take a stand and toe the party line.

She joined the Labour Party in August 1976 but when voting against the Government's Emergency legislation in September 1976, Mrs. Robinson was still not a member of the Labour Parliamentary Party. The following month she was admitted and unanimously welcomed by the members of the Parliamentary Party in Leinster House.

In the week Mrs. Robinson's letter of application came before the Parliamentary Party it had also received a letter from Dr. David Thornley, her fellow Trinity academic. He was seeking re-admission to the Parliamentary Party from which he had been expelled for attending an Easter commemoration organised by the Provisionals. Dr. Thornley, like Senator Robinson, was also opposed to the Coalition's Emergency legislation.

Had they both been members of the Parliamentary Party at that period they would have been expelled for their action. Abstention was the only form of protest open to a Parliamentary Party member. At the time of Mrs. Robinson's application for membership, Labour was considering introducing a regulation under which deputies and senators would be expelled for abstention.

During Mrs. Robinson's first month of membership of the Labour Parliamentary Party, the coalition administration found itself caught in the eye of one of the most embarrassing political storms the country had witnessed since the Arms Trial in 1970. At its centre was the Emergency legislation which Mrs. Robinson so strongly opposed.

On Thursday 21 October 1976 the Leader of the Opposition, Jack

Lynch, rose in the Dáil to move a motion requesting the resignation of the Minister for Defence, Patrick Donegan. Mr. Donegan, in an unscripted statement to members of the Defence Forces in Mullingar, Co. Westmeath, had referred to the President of Ireland, Cearbhall Ó Dálaigh, as a "thundering disgrace" or words to that effect. The reason the Minister had come to such an extraordinary conclusion about the Head of State and Commander-in-Chief of the Defence Forces was that the President had referred the controversial Emergency legislation to the Supreme Court, as was his right under the Constitution. Mr. Lynch told the House that the statement was of the gravest importance coming from a Minister of the Government, reflecting on the integrity, capacity, and constitutional status of the Head of State from whom the Minister had received his Seal of Office. Coming from a Government Minister, Mr. Lynch said, such a statement was neither understandable nor forgivable.

But forgiven it was. Mr. Donegan's party leader, Liam Cosgrave, and the majority of his colleagues were unwilling to see the remark as anything more than a *faux pas*. The Minister was not sacked but merely moved sideways, being replaced in Defence by Mrs. Robinson's old adversary in the contraception debate, Oliver J. Flanagan.

When President Ó Dálaigh resigned over the affair, the wind of a general election was blowing full strength around Leinster House.

In February 1977 the Labour Party's Organisation Committee met to consider how best it should prepare for the election. Four Dublin constituencies came under special scrutiny - Artane, Cabra, Finglas, and Rathmines West. The latter constituency was well worth the special attention of the Party strategists, for in it all three main parties had an almost equal chance of taking the third seat.

The political commentators were predicting a coalition win in the general election but many predicted that Labour's share of the vote in Dublin would fall yet again. The all too public dissension within the Party was a factor which gave the leadership due cause for concern. In the run-up to the selection conventions and the election itself, Mary Robinson became embroiled in the public washing of at least some of the Party's dirty linen.

Labour had a number of advantages on its side facing into the general election. James Tully, the Minister for Local Government, had carved up the constituencies in what became known as the "Tullymander". Its effect should have given Labour the chance of winning seats where it might otherwise have been expected to lose them. In the capital's newer residential suburbs, and in the growing ranks of the Party's middle-class supporters, its standing had been enhanced somewhat by its years in coalition.

It was inevitable, however, that the association with the Coalition carried more disadvantages than advantages for a party anxious to win a wide cross-section of support. The recession of 1974-5 and the oil crisis that went with it, were dealt with by the introduction of deflationary policies: a wealth tax was introduced; there was an attempt to tax farmers; the Taoiseach voted against his own Government's Contraception Bill; the Coalition's Northern policy seemed to lack direction; the heavy hand of law and order policy was much in evidence.

Maurice Manning, in his essay in *Ireland at the Polls: The Dáil Election of 1977* sums up the position of the Labour Party at this time:

"...The years 1973-1977 can be seen as mixed years for Labour. The party participated more extensively and more vigorously in Government than at any previous time in its history, and undoubtedly the prestige of office buoyed up many of its activists, certainly in the early stages. Substantial advances were made in a number of areas with which Labour was associated - especially welfare legislation, natural resources, and labour legislation. By-elections and local elections showed continuing support... But undoubtedly, too, the experience of office exacerbated tensions within the Party, raised uncomfortable questions of party identity and long-term strategy, and exposed the nature of Labour's dilemma: how to maintain credibility with its natural supporters, the workers, while remaining in a coalition led by the conservative leader of a basically conservative party, especially at a time of unemployment and inflation."

A majority of the electorate was indeed well disposed towards the Coalition's policy on social welfare. While the Government's Northern and security policies were not popular, their position on both issues was ahead of the Fianna Fáil alternatives in the opinion polls.

The economic policies of the Government took a hammering in polls taken in late 1976. Two-thirds of the electorate were critical of the Coalition's handling of the country's economic ills. A year before the 1977 general election Fianna Fáil gained very little from that particularly high level of public dissatisfaction.

Just before the general election the Government regained some ground and most political commentators, even on polling day itself, gave the Coalition the edge over Fianna Fáil. The general perception was that international rather than domestic factors were responsible for Ireland's economic malaise and Fianna Fáil had no panacea for those ills.

Labour was confident as it faced into the 1977 general election that it would emerge reasonably unscathed at the hands of an electorate which, if the opinion polls could be trusted, looked like returning a Coalition Government to Leinster House. But the Party was very much aware of the tactical groundwork that needed to be done in key constituencies if it was to take full advantage of the "Tullymander". One such constituency was Rathmines West where Mary Robinson made the first of her two attempts to secure a Dáil seat.

Just how marginal the new constituency was could be seen from the result of the final count in the 1973 general election in the reasonably similar four-seater constituency of Dublin South Central when John O'Donovan of Labour failed to take a seat by a margin of a mere 786 votes.

The new constituency of Rathmines West extended from the well-manicured lawns of sedate Rathgar in the east, to the unemployment belt of working-class Crumlin in the west; bordered by the Grand Canal on its northern extremity and the River Dodder on its southern, it also contained the warren that was flatland Rathmines and the residential heartlands of Harold's Cross and Kimmage.

Fianna Fáil and Fine Gael were determined to take that much sought-after third seat in Rathmines West. Fine Gael's front runner was Finance Minister Richie Ryan who, despite a poor popularity rating nationally, was popular in the constituency itself, where he had a well-earned reputation for working relentlessly for his constituents. His running mates were Cllr. Seán Kelly and former Lord Mayor of Dublin James O'Keeffe.

Fianna Fáil also fielded three candidates. Their team was headed by Ben Briscoe who had topped the poll in the area in the 1974 local elections. His running mates were Gerard Brady, whose father, Philip Brady, was the outgoing TD, and Noreen Slattery. Miss Slattery worked in the Irish Management Institute as an administrative assistant and had some backing from the Women's Political Association. Fianna Fáil did not expect her to take a seat, but what it did expect her to take was as large as possible a proportion of the women's vote from Mary Robinson.

The back-room wrangling that went into selecting Labour's candidates in the constituency is a very good example, *in vacuo*, of the broader internal wrangling that beset the Party as a whole at this time.

The strategy in the constituency was for Labour to run a two-man ticket. The front runner was to be Cllr. Mick Collins who was a member of the Executive of the Workers' Union of Ireland. He had polled well for Labour in the local elections taking the seat vacated by the former Deputy Lord Mayor of Dublin, Dermot O'Rourke.

Collins was seen as a solid constituency worker with a reliable support base in the working-class suburb of Crumlin.

The running mate tipped to appear with Mick Collins on the Labour ticket was the constituency vice-chairman, Dr. David Neligan. Dr. Neligan was a dentist with a large practice in the area and was a well-known local figure. He also had a national profile as chairman of the Resources Protection Campaign and was regularly involved, in that capacity, in high-profile media debates. He had been a member of the Labour Party since the 1960s and had been unaffected by the various internal upheavals which the Party experienced before entering

100

into coalition with Fine Gael. He was an active member of Left Liaison, a group within the Party which was bitterly opposed to what it saw as the betrayal of the left-wing policies adopted by the Party in the late 1960s. It was expected that he would receive a substantial amount of transfers from the Sinn Féin candidate, Eric Byrne.

This well-made plan was knocked rather sharply on the head by the arrival in the constituency of Labour's most recent and most distinguished new recruit, Trinity senator Mary Robinson. The Party establishment saw the advantage of having such a candidate on the ticket. She would not only lend the weight of a national personality to the contest in a key constituency like Rathmines West, but she would also be likely to attract the middle-of-the-road voter in the more middle-class areas of the constituency. For Mrs. Robinson herself, her place on the ticket brought her one step nearer to fulfilling part of her own personal career agenda - a seat in Dáil Éireann. Her first step into that quagmire of grassroots politics was, however, a baptism of fire for the Trinity senator.

The first task facing any potential candidate seeking a party nomination for a Dáil election is a quick assessment of the Constituency Convention arithmetic. With an eye to that future task, Mrs. Robinson had been associated, in December 1976, with the formation of two new Labour Party branches in the constituency. These were at Neagh Road and Leinster Road. It was alleged, most notably by David Neligan, in the bulletin of Left Liaison, that what Mrs. Robinson was engaged in was the creation of so-called "paper branches" whose only function was to bolster a particular candidate's chances of making it past the winning-post at a Constituency Selection Convention.

An unholy row followed the refusal of the Rathmines Constituency Council of the Labour Party to ratify the branches by a vote of 25 to 1. The rules stated that a branch had to be in existence for six months prior to a selection convention. The matter was passed to the Party's Administrative Council which came up with the novel solution that months referred not to calendar but to lunar months. In other words six lunar months - 24 weeks - was sufficient to legitimate a new branch and it could then play its part in a Selection Convention.

The allegations against Mary Robinson did not stop at the issue of "paper branches". It was also alleged that she was a "tame stooge" of Party head office who had been offered several other possible nominations before settling for Rathmines West. It was suggested in the bulletin of Left Liaison that she had been offered Artane but refused it. She had been invited to seek nominations in Cavan-Monaghan, and the James Connolly Branch in Balbriggan had also written to her asking if she would consider seeking a nomination under its auspices, but Artane did not feature in the equation.

Perhaps the most potentially damaging allegation made against her was that it was her intention to drop in and out of the Rathmines West constituency on her way to the European Parliament.

Exasperated and annoyed by the coverage that the allegations were receiving in the media, Mrs. Robinson did her best to effect what damage limitation she could on a local level in Rathmines, by talking, on a personal basis, to branch officers and ordinary members. She also took the unusual step of giving the matter a national airing in the letters pages of *Hibernia*, where she wrote a blistering refutation of all the above mentioned allegations.

"The stories are so completely without foundation and so way-out," she wrote in the letter published on Friday 29 April, "that it is hard to believe that I need to reject them one by one, but they have received some publicity and may have raised a doubt. If I had wanted to further my own career in a narrow sense, I would have been intelligent enough not to join the Labour Party. Careers are furthered more rapidly in either of the other two political parties."

"I realise," she continued, "that this is a bitter and disillusioned time for the Labour Party, but that does not justify using tactics which are a combination of lies and hypocrisy to block my candidature..."

The letter contained a point-by-point rebuttal of the main allegations made against her. On the question of "paper branches" in Rathmines West she denied that the two new branches she was involved with came under the category of "paper". She named the secretary of the Neagh Road branch as Mrs. Dodo Taylor and said it was already active on local issues such as plans to widen the Lower Kimmage Road. She said the Leinster Road branch was already circulating a newsletter and it had recently been addressed by Senator John Horgan on Labour's education policy.

"The reality," Mrs. Robinson wrote, "is that the Labour Party in the Rathmines West constituency has two active branches which are gaining support from people living in that constituency. Supporting the development of such branches is a legitimate, and indeed vital, activity for anyone who wishes to seek a nomination in the area."

The one fact that may have weakened Mary Robinson's case was the inclusion of Nick Robinson among the ranks of the recruits in the newly formed Leinster Road branch. Nick Robinson had not been a political activist, even during his student days at Trinity, and his interests were clearly those of the aesthete and not those of the Labour Party political hack. It would, however, even in the bitter back-biting atmosphere of those Rathmines West days, have taken a very brave soul to argue that the two were mutually exclusive. Party records also show that Mrs. Robinson's secretary, Ann Lane, and an old family friend, Declan Geraghty - who had worked on the Senate campaigns - had both been recruited into the Leinster Road branch.

Mary Robinson bluntly denied that she was using Rathmines West as a stepping-stone to Brussels. A rumour had been circulated to the effect that she was seen canvassing Labour Party branches in her native Mayo with an eye to the Direct Elections to the European Parliament.

That letter to *Hibernia* was more than an open refutation of what she saw as Neligan-inspired attacks on her possible candidature in Rathmines West. In the letter the new Labour Parliamentary Party member described just where she stood in relation to it thus:

"...I want to state categorically that I consider myself to be on the left of the Labour Parliamentary Party, and that is where I intend to remain. My record makes this clear. I voted against the Declaration of Emergency and the Emergency Powers Bill 1976, and I have consistently championed the cause of civil liberties in Ireland. I have advocated radical family law reform, and fought hard for a comprehensive scheme of family planning. I have championed equality for women and criticised the Social Welfare Act 1977 for refusing to remove the blatant discrimination in qualifications for unemployment assistance between men and women. I shall continue to make this contribution, using my skills as a lawyer and my concern for civil liberty as well as my commitment to socialism in Ireland."

All the theory in the world would be of little service to Mary Robinson if she wanted to secure a party nomination and a Dáil seat. She set about the day-to-day practicalities of political life by establishing two advice "clinics", one in Mount Pleasant Avenue and the other on the Lower Kimmage Road. It was run-of-the-mill stuff but she was, naturally, as a lawyer, quite useful to her potential constituents on a wide range of legal matters. Her advice was always given after impeccable research into the problem on which her advice was sought but, according to Party workers, it sometimes went over the heads of the people seeking it, and the Trinity academic appeared somewhat stiff and formal while delivering it.

The somewhat untidy Labour stage of Rathmines West was now set for Mary Robinson to make her entry in her bid for a Dáil nomination.

It was quite clear to the election strategists at Labour HQ that Rathmines West could not have three Labour candidates on the ticket.

In her own branch, Rathmines, more than 75 per cent of the membership favoured Mary Robinson as their candidate. Her opponents were not impressed, arguing that since she controlled the branch, this hardly represented a constituency-wide trend.

The "paper branch" allegation reared its ugly head above the parapet again, only to have it blasted off by Party HQ. This time the tables were turned on the Neligan camp. Mrs. Robinson said that she regarded the pro-Neligan, Mount Drummond branch, as one of the dreaded "paper" variety. Mount Drummond and another pro-Neligan branch, Harold's Cross, were investigated by Labour's Organisation

104

Committee. The Committee's chairman, Barry Desmond, was called in, and having talked to officials involved, he gave his imprimatur to both branches.

In March 1976 three of Labour's eight branches in Rathmines West supported the candidature of David Neligan; two were backing Mick Collins while Mary Robinson and John Throne of the left-wing "Militant" had the support of one branch each. That left one branch uncommitted. Aware of the tensions in the constituency, Labour Party HQ was refusing the local organisations' demands for a Selection Convention at that time. It was mooted, however, that when the Convention took place three candidates would be selected. When it did take place, in late May, the convention decided by a vote of 20 votes to 12 to put forward only two candidates.

Mary Robinson received only four votes out of the 32. David Neligan with 12 and Michael Collins with 14 were selected to stand for Labour in Rathmines West. John Throne received only two votes.

With an eye on that third seat, Labour's Administrative Council decided to add Mary Robinson's name to the list. The Council, as *The Irish Times* put it, "was acting constitutionally, though breaking the rules". David Neligan's supporters were furious at the decision and Dr. Neligan withdrew his name from the slate with some sharp criticism of how the Party exercised democracy.

Denis Byrne, writing in *Hibernia* before the election, summed up both Labour's dilemma, and a view of Mrs. Robinson that was prevalent in certain quarters of Rathmines West in the run-up to the general election:

"Mary Robinson's intervention has presented the local Labour Party with a difficult dilemma: she would certainly add prestige to the Party ticket and attract a middle-of-the-road vote, but her presence could create the sort of internal divisions which cost the Party the seat in 1973. Again the questions must be posed, is her conversion to socialism a genuine political rebirth or is she merely using the Labour Party as a flag of convenience? If elected would she continue to represent the constituency or would her obvious European ambitions result in the

Rathmines Labour Party having to find another candidate in time for the succeeding election."

Notwithstanding the row that heralded her entry into the contest, Senator Robinson was expected to poll well. The constituency had more than the usual spread of middle-class, educated, liberal voters, and the voting trend there, that had benefited Fine Gael's John Kelly over Labour's John O'Donovan in 1973, was expected to go her way. The Party also expected her to do well in the more traditional Labour stronghold of Crumlin. However, her running mate Michael Collins - "a firm believer in the rights of all workers" as his election blurb read - was expected to do better there.

Polling was set for Bloomsday - 16 June. "Happy Bloomsday", a sign in the window of the Labour HQ in Rathmines proclaimed. But all was far from happy behind that façade. David Neligan and his supporters decamped across the river Liffey to Artane and Finglas, leaving Mrs. Robinson to battle with Michael Collins for control of what remained of the Party election machine. Just how bitter that battle was could be seen when Mr. Collins's transfers were counted. The failure of an effective transfer of those votes was to cost Labour the third seat.

Mary Robinson's supporters put up, what one canvasser called, "a spirited performance". They sometimes met with disappointment in unexpected quarters. One canvasser said he was surprised to find Douglas Gageby of The Irish Times less than enthusiastic.

As with every election in her public career, her Mayo family travelled from the West to support her. Together with what could be mustered from Labour's own constituency team, Mary Robinson's usual team of election workers were marshalled, and they were joined by Trinity and UCD students - many of whom were not even Labour supporters, but admired the liberal stand Mrs. Robinson had taken in the Senate on a whole range of issues. They included people like Antoinette Quinn of Trinity's English Department, Edward McParland, the distinguished art historian, and W.E. Vaughan of Trinity's History Department.

Sometimes the most unlikely people turned up to lend a hand. Nigel Burton, a High Tory Englishman who lectured in music at Trinity offered his support. According to one election worker, it often took the form of tearing down the opposition's posters.

There were moments of light relief. At one stage during the campaign a rumour circulated that Mary Robinson had the backing of the Egyptian Government. This surfaced after canvassers approached a character in Rathmines who was a frequenter of Trinity common rooms and known to carry an Egyptian passport. When asked if he would vote for Mary Robinson he took the matter so seriously that he announced that "Egypt is backing Mrs. Robinson!"

Support meetings took place in the home of Maura O'Dea of CHERISH, in Lower Kimmage Road. On the canvass it was felt by her supporters that, even though she was coming across on the doorsteps as aloof, stiff and formal, the fact that so many of the voters knew exactly who she was, and what she stood for, would see her through to take the third seat. It very nearly did.

Mary Robinson was defeated on the eighth and final count by a margin as narrow as 406 votes.

64 per cent of the 41,679 voters entitled to vote, did so. The quota was 6,694. On the first count the situation was as follows:

Byrne, E.	(IND)	1,148
Brady, G.	(FF)	6,064
Ryan, R.	(FG)	5,486
Briscoe, B.	(FF)	5,149
ROBINSON, M.	(LAB)	2,854
Collins, M.	(LAB)	2,377
O'Keeffe, J.	(FG)	1,311
Kelly, S.	(FG)	1,258
Slattery, N.	(FF)	1,126

On the eighth and final count with the distribution of Collins's votes the situation was:

Briscoe	+349	6,488
ROBINSON	+2,330	6,082

The irony for the Coalition was that the "Tullymander" worked in Fianna Fáil's favour giving it the biggest parliamentary majority in the history of the State. Fianna Fáil won 50.6 per cent of the first preference votes and 84 of the 148 seats in the Dáil, Fine Gael 30.5 per cent and 43 seats and Labour 11.6 per cent and 17 seats. On paper the idea of the "Tullymander" was brilliant; in practice it failed to live up to expectation. Reducing the size of the constituencies left the Government open to the English electoral principle of the "swing", whereby even a relatively small change in public mood can wipe out a Government majority. Churchill had fallen victim to it in 1945 as have successive British governments.

Labour, in spite of its obvious difficulties incurred through internal division and infighting, came close enough to matching its performance in the 1973 general election in terms of votes and seats.

The tragedy from Labour's point of view - and Mary Robinson was but one of many victims of this - was that despite the swing to Fianna Fáil, it could have made a net gain in seats if it had managed to contain the Party squabbling. Two Labour Ministers, Conor Cruise O'Brien and Justin Keating, lost their seats in Dublin. The mastermind of the "Tullymander", former Local Government Minister, Jim Tully, came close to losing his seat in Meath. The vote of the Party Leader, Brendan Corish, dropped in Co. Wexford. The Party's General Secretary failed to win a seat in Dublin. For the Party leadership there was much soul searching to be done.

Mary Robinson did her soul searching rather quickly. She had every reason to be pleased with her performance as a first time out candidate. She announced that she would seek re-election to the Senate on the Trinity College panel. She said that if the Coalition had been returned she would not have sought re-election on that panel, as she would have had to take the Government Whip in the House. She said that since Fianna Fáil had been returned with such a large majority, there was an important job to be done in the Senate, scrutinising Government legislation. If she sought precedent for her decision, there was, of course, the precedent of Dr. Noel Browne and Owen Sheehy Skeffington, who had both been returned on the Trinity Panel while members of the Labour Party.

The challenging circumstances in which she found herself in Rathmines West had made Mary Robinson one of the hardened campaigners of national politics. Now, with the benefit of considerable experience at the coal-face, she headed into yet another contest.

13

LABOUR SENATOR

Much soul-searching followed Labour's performance in the 1977 general election. In the fetid atmosphere of the election post-mortem, Mrs. Robinson did not escape the wrath of some of her Party colleagues. David Thornley - who had polled over 8,400 first preference votes in 1969, survived in 1973 and lost his deposit in 1977 - rounded on her in public.

Within days of the announcement of the final result he attacked her for attempting to do a deal with David Neligan which would have moved the Dublin dentist sideways in Rathmines West as she advanced onwards on her march towards Europe. Dr. Thornley also questioned her position in seeking a Senate seat for Trinity as a member of the Labour Party. Mary Robinson dismissed Dr. Thornley's allegations in yet another letter to *The Irish Times* on 2 July 1977. The spectre of that alleged "deal" hung uncomfortably close even long after the election. She announced in that letter that she would stand for the Senate in the Trinity constituency as a member of the Labour Party. Conor Cruise O'Brien was also standing in the Trinity constituency as a Labour Party member.

Until the 1977 Senate election there had been a tendency amongst the voters in the two University constituencies to resist party political candidates who offered themselves for election. In 1977 this changed.

Under Article 18 of the Irish Constitution, the Senate elections must be held within 90 days of the date of dissolution of the Dáil. The 1977 campaign began earlier than expected and counting of votes was scheduled to commence on 17 August. As is often the case in

Senate elections, canvassing began even before the close of nominations. With so many Coalition TDs (including three ex-ministers) without seats in the Dáil after the 1977 election debacle, competition for Senate nominations was quite intense. The three ex-ministers, Patrick Cooney, Justin Keating and Conor Cruise O'Brien were all expected to take seats.

For her 1977 campaign, Mary Robinson appointed her friend Dr. Mary Henry (now a senator herself) as her election agent. Dr. Henry remained her election agent for all but the last of Mrs. Robinson's Senate campaigns. They would later have a disagreement over Mrs. Robinson's departure from the Labour Party. The announcement had been made to the media before Dr. Henry knew anything about it, and this caused a temporary rift in their friendship. But for the 1977 campaign the usual team was assembled in Wellington Place and Mrs. Robinson sat down to write her election address.

Her circumstances had changed considerably since she last addressed the Trinity electorate. She was now a member of the Labour Party and would take the Party Whip in the Senate if returned for Trinity. This needed some explanation.

She wrote in her address that, while she still valued the position of the Independent as an appropriate stance from which to judge issues on their merits, gradually she had come to believe that that was no longer enough. Her political commitment had deepened, she said, and she was convinced that she could make a more substantial contribution within the overall political framework as part of a team.

She repeated what she had already said about not taking the Government Whip, if the Coalition had been returned to office. She again stressed how there was now a need for experienced senators to ensure that the Senate did not become a rubber stamp for the Government with the largest majority in the history of the State. She concluded her explanation with an appeal:

"I can understand and respect the views of those of my supporters who regret what they see as the abandonment of an independent position. I ask them to consider that I have not in any real sense sacrificed my independence or theirs by taking the Labour Party Whip. I have simply, I believe, strengthened that independence within the scheme and coherence of an honoured political tradition. And I believe that Trinity, with its subtle understanding through its own traditions of thought and activities, has always shown, through its graduates, a particular sympathy for the conscientious decision. Mine has been such a one; and I ask for their support for it. If re-elected, I shall continue as I have done for the past eight years, to scrutinise legislation carefully, to speak out doggedly on minority issues, to advocate reform where there is need for reform and to point out injustices and discriminations where these exist."

As she faced into the campaign Mary Robinson was aware that she had built up a substantial support base after her resounding success in the 1973 Senate election, when she had topped the poll. Fresh from her defeat in Rathmines West she was also aware that there was no room for complacency. While most political commentators saw her seat as a safe one, some felt that her membership of the Labour Party would alienate the more conservative Protestant voters who had supported her in the previous two contests. Mary Robinson was determined that the confidence she won in 1969 and in 1973 would accrue to her again in 1977.

"We have the highest unemployment rate in the EEC," Mrs. Robinson reminded the electors of Trinity College, in her election address. "We have a crippling inflation rate. Our young people are without outlets for their energy or opportunities to use their skills to the benefit of themselves and the community." The address was beginning to read like an Opposition condemnation of the years of Coalition Government.

"If we are not to lose their confidence," she continued, "if we are not to allow another drain of our skilled and unskilled workers into other employment markets - a trend which is already beginning - we must discover the structures to contain and amplify our wealth, and the courage to develop these structures for the benefit of all the people." In every one of her election addresses to the Trinity

113

constituency, Mary Robinson gave very high priority to the issue which was eventually to lead to her parting of the ways with the Labour Party. Trinity College, with its large intake of students from Northern Ireland, was particularly aware of the problems facing both communities in the North. Northern Ireland was an issue with which Mrs. Robinson had been concerned since she entered public life, but it was not an issue with which the general public would have associated her.

That situation has changed considerably since she has become President of Ireland, and has led to the first major controversy of her presidency - her meeting and handshake with Gerry Adams of Sinn Féin, during her visit to West Belfast in June 1993.

Her public approach to the Northern question in the '70s was marked mainly by her contributions to the constitutional debate. Those contributions tended to be of a somewhat intellectual nature and therefore not headline-making. Her public stand on the internment question did, of course, make the headlines, but not until she became embroiled in a public argument with Conor Cruise O'Brien. She was also critical in the late '70s of the lack of opportunity to debate the Northern question in the Senate and she called for a statutory report on developments in relation to Northern Ireland to be delivered twice a year to the Dáil and the Senate.

"I do not need to remind anyone of the continual brutalities and inhumanities of the situation," she told the Trinity electorate. "I shall confine myself to one brutality, less seen, yet quite crucial. This is the way in which - despite public avowals of horror - we continue to brutalise the situation by assuming inflexible cultural patterns and dogmatic notions of "Irishness". The battlefield of the North on which we can fight most effectively, I am sure, is that of its cultural identity and our changing perception of it. We cannot at this distance alter the barbarity and absurdity of individual deaths. We can and we should be looking for a flexible and generous interpretation of nationality for the whole of this island which, by removing rigid definitions of identity, would remove the necessity to fight for and against such definitions."

The basic thrust of Mrs. Robinson's election address was

concentrated on her legislative and public speaking record. But having considered the issues mentioned above she also included two paragraphs on the environment, which didn't really say very much, but certainly indicated that she was aware of the growing importance of the environmental lobby, especially in the University Senate constituencies.

This time out she was nominated by the Trinity and Cambridge-educated mathematics professor, Thomas David Spearman, and, as always, the second name on the list was her father-in-law, Howard Robinson. She rather sensibly shortened the published list of her assentors to eight. Opening the Douglas Hyde Gallery in Trinity, Jack Lynch remarked that Trinity had now entered "the mainstream of Irish life". The Register of Electors for the Trinity constituency now reflected this, and it no longer benefited a Senate candidate to append a list of establishment Protestant names to an election address. Amongst the eight assentors were broadcaster John Bowman, and poet Brendan Kennelly.

Ballot papers were sent out to all 8,007 voters on 15 July and were to be returned by 17 August for counting in the Public Theatre, known to generations of Trinity graduates as the "Exam Hall".

There were 12 candidates in quest of the three Trinity seats. The front runners were Conor Cruise O'Brien, Mary Robinson and Trevor West. Names that would later be prominent on the Irish political stage were also in the field - Alan Shatter, David Norris, Shane Ross and Catherine McGuinness. Antiques dealer Willie Dillon, the brother of the Robinson's future Sandford Road neighbour, Val Dillon, was also a candidate.

The valid poll was 5,298. There were 115 spoiled votes and the quota was 1,354. The result of the first count gave the top three candidates the following votes:

O'Brien, Conor Cruise	1,245
West, Trevor	1,057
ROBINSON, Mary	900

No candidate was elected until the sixth count, when Dr. O'Brien exceeded the quota, reaching a total of 1,378 votes. On the seventh count, Trevor West took the second seat with 1,407 votes and on the eighth count Mary Robinson was elected when she reached 1,542 votes.

On that warm August afternoon, in the relaxed atmosphere of College Park, a confident Trevor West captained his own XI in a cricket match against Bangor, Co. Down, while Mary Robinson waited to take the third and final seat. She withdrew quietly to consider the implications of coming home, in third place, in the Trinity constituency.

It can only have been a disappointment to Mary Robinson to have reverted to the same position she had found herself in, on her first electoral outing in 1969. Her share of the first preference vote had dropped substantially since the 1973 Senate election. It was time for quiet reflection.

The overall picture in the make-up of the 1977 Senate was not as encouraging for Fianna Fáil as it was in the Dáil. The Government won control of the House by a majority of two seats over the combined opposition of Fine Gael, Labour and four Independents. Two former Coalition Ministers, Paddy Cooney and Conor Cruise O'Brien, headed the poll in their separate constituencies and another former Minister, Justin Keating, won a seat on the Agriculture Panel. Labour had seven senators in the newly returned House.

Mary Robinson began the process of reflection by looking first of all at the condition of the Party she had so recently joined.

Frank Cluskey replaced Brendan Corish as Labour leader after the leadership election of 1977. "We should be more openly aggressive about being socialist," Mr. Cluskey said to his followers, when introducing the policy document *The Socialist Dimension* in 1978 - before he addressed his first Party Conference as leader - "not apologetic; but we must be realistic. People will not vote for pie in the sky - they want an overall, ultimate vision, but they also want action relevant to their day to day problems."

Mary Robinson's party was engaged in a campaign to enlarge and improve its political base and to involve new elements such as Labour

Youth and recently established elements like the National Labour Women's Council; and to revitalise the party's links with well-established elements like the Trade Unions.

Frank Cluskey was anxious that what should emerge under his leadership, as the Party faced into the 1980s, was a view of Labour as a party which held firmly to the principles of democratic socialism. There would be dissenters who would find unpalatable such watered-down socialism. Some would leave only to return and resume their political activity, others would stay and be critical from within, some would abandon the Party never to return. Within nine years of joining it Mary Robinson would leave the Labour Party on what she considered a firm and principled stand. But what of her attitude as she sat on the Party benches in the Senate?

In a number of interviews which she gave in the late 1970s, she had some hard things to say about the state of the Labour Party. In an *Irish Times* interview with Geraldine Kennedy, in July 1979, she said she felt the Labour Party had put people off socialism. The Party had failed, she told Miss Kennedy, to put socialist proposals for the economic and social structure of Ireland which would be deeply relevant to the Irish people. "It had failed," she explained, "because it had borrowed a language that is more suitable to an urban society like Britain, and it puts people off."

"I don't believe that the Labour Party is, as yet, putting forward policies in a language that people around the country relate to their lives. The word 'socialism' is still alien, un-Irish and, for a lot of people, not a way to look at the economic and social structure that affects their everyday lives."

What the Party needed to do, she said, was to re-define socialism in Irish terms. "One of the bad images of socialism in Ireland," she continued, "is that it would be an anonymous State organ ruling all our lives in an inefficient way."

It was a pessimistic Mary Robinson who told Geraldine Kennedy that the type of social discontent she saw in Ireland had created three distinct streams in society.

There were the better off, she said, who were regarded by the Government as a productive elite. Then there was the middle and low-paid workers who were not getting the type of wage rises to allow them to keep pace with the ever-increasing mortgage and household bills which create pressure within families. Then there was what she called the forgotten 25 per cent who were living in conditions of really grinding, desperate and de-humanising poverty.

There was a clear indication at the end of the 1970s of how Mary Robinson's role had changed since she entered active politics. "I am now more inclined to relate anything I do," she told Geraldine Kennedy, "to the overall economic and social context." This was quite evident in the type of issues she was speaking on in the Senate. Unlike some of the other University senators she did not disappear to the academic cloisters when the somewhat dry detail of social legislation was being debated. She did her best to make a significant contribution to all types of social legislation. A list of Mary Robinson's public speaking engagements for the mid to late 1970s indicates that she attempted to gain first hand knowledge of the social issues she spoke of in the Senate by speaking directly to organisations involved in a wide range of those social questions - the unemployed, unmarried mothers, old people's organisations, travellers.

While her concern for the rights of the individual was uppermost in her mind, she also realised early on in public life that such platforms gave her almost unlimited access to column inches of newspaper coverage. The scant attention paid by the media in general to the proceedings of the Senate meant it was, for the most part, a waste of time making important pronouncements on social issues in the chamber. Outside the confines of Leinster House, Mary Robinson was the most reported senator in the country. Even her most bland utterances on the most obvious of social discriminations, like the condition of old folks' housing in inner city Dublin, invariably made one or other of the national newspapers. Any organisation in the country which sought publicity for its cause needed to look no further than the inclusion of Mary Robinson on its platform to be reasonably

118

sure of media coverage.

One of the organisations with which she had a close and long-standing personal association was CHERISH. The organisation was founded to help unmarried parents. It highlighted the discriminations against the single parent, all of which stood contrary to the constitutional guarantee that "All citizens shall, as human persons, be held equal before the law". Mary Robinson became interested after one of the founders of CHERISH, Maura O'Dea, came to see her in her rooms in Merrion Square.

Throughout the 1970s Mary Robinson battled harder than any public figure in Ireland to remove the legal and social discriminations which attached to the status of the illegitimate child. On 13 February 1975 she withdrew her Illegitimate Children (Maintenance & Succession) Bill 1974, but only in view of the fact that the Minister for Justice had promised the early introduction of a Family Law Reform Bill which would cover the ground with which she was most concerned. She withdrew the Bill with the stern warning that unless the Minister lived up to his promise she would introduce a new and improved Private Member's Bill.

She later had considerable influence over the drafting of a Private Member's Bill (The Sixth Amendment of the Constitution Bill 1978) which Labour introduced in the Dáil. The measure had three objectives: to remove the status of illegitimacy, to extend the category of children who could be adopted to include children who had been abandoned or seriously ill-treated by their married parents, and to ensure the constitutionality of the powers of the Adoption Board. The measure was defeated in the House but the Minister for Justice introduced a Government Bill dealing only with the third of these issues. It was subsequently approved in a referendum.

Now in her third period as senator - not quite an elder of the House but one of its senior members - she was more critical than ever of the way the Senate was forced to conduct its business. Her views on this became well known soon after her election in 1969. She made her famous "I am under-employed" remark, referred to earlier, at that time. Speaking to the motion, "That the Senate is an Unnecessary Extravagance", at UCD's Law Society on 6 November 1975, she had remarked how it had become fashionable to air that view of the Senate at least once a year, and usually during the artificially long summer recess. It was a particularly timely motion that November when the House remained adjourned for a longer than usual recess because of the by-election in West Mayo caused by the death of Fine Gael's Henry Kelly.

There was little use in a chamber which was effectively a rubber stamp for the Government, she told her UCD audience. She made the case, yet again, for the Senate to exploit its vocational nature through the establishment of specialist committees which would give a different and enriching consideration to Government measures.

As a general rule the Senate meets only when there is Government business to be discussed. This is as much the fault of successive oppositions as it is that of successive Governments. Through her regular demands for time in the House for the discussion of Private Member's business, and through regular criticism outside it, Mary Robinson tried, with little success, to alter that situation. By the time the Senate got round to celebrating its 40th birthday in 1978, she was so exasperated with the cumbersome way it went about conducting its business that she said, in an *Irish Times* feature on the anniversary, that she considered it an institution that was too expensive, met too rarely and used too few of its powers to justify the amount of money and space it took up. Her strongest criticism of the Senate was of its standing orders which compelled it to approach legislation in the same slow mechanical way in which the Dáil did. Her view of the House was that it remained, on its 40th birthday, the Dáil's "poor brother". She concluded that as senators they were members of a club that had too much tolerance for the rules of the club.

Mrs. Robinson came into conflict with those rules on a number of occasions. One of the most notable was on 15 April 1981 when she was suspended from the House. The Labour senator had taken up the case of Mrs. Mary Courtney, a mother of four, who was the first woman usher appointed to Leinster House. Mrs. Courtney had been transferred to the Department of Labour against her will and without proper explanation. Mrs. Robinson had pressed the Cathaoirleach, Seamus Doolan, to explain why a motion of hers on the transfer of the woman from Leinster House, was not being accepted for debate. Senator Doolan said the matter was not suitable for discussion on the adjournment on the grounds that it contained matters of "personal imputation". Senator Robinson said the removal of the first female usher in the Oireachtas appeared to be discrimination. Mrs. Robinson pressed the Chair repeatedly to give an explanation of his ruling. She was finally "named" by the Leader of the House, Eoin Ryan, and expelled by a vote of 21 to 13.

A month later, and just a few days short of her 37th birthday, Senator Robinson was out of the House again - this time of her own free will. During the debate on the second stage of the Prisons Bill 1980, she objected to the detention of civilian prisoners then in military custody at the Curragh Camp. After particular difficulties in prisons like Mountjoy, where there had been serious riots in 1972, the Minister for Justice transferred those he saw as the trouble makers to military custody. Mary Robinson was totally opposed to such a move, and in the course of making her views known she crossed swords with an old army man, Fianna Fáil senator Joe Dowling. He took Mrs. Robinson's position to be a slur on the Army and he said so in the House. She made repeated objections to the Chair about his remark, but to no avail, so she left the chamber in protest.

Mary Robinson's contribution to the Senate in this period, was as active on debates on Government Bills and Motions, as it was on her own legislative initiatives. Since her election the range was quite impressive: Family Planning Bill 1973 and 1974; Illegitimate Children (Maintenance and Succession) Bill 1974; The Companies (Amendment) Bill 1975. Motions and Adjournment Debates included: Demolition of Dublin Houses, 1975; Rules for the Government of Prisons, 1976; Equal Pay, 1976; and, rather amusingly, Revenue Commissioners' Notices.

On 23 March 1977 she reminded the House that although the *McGee* case of 1973 had decided that the ban on contraceptive devices for private use was unconstitutional, three-and-a-half years later they were still included as prohibited items in the Revenue Commissioners' notices for the guidance of residents and visitors to Ireland. As she told her Trinity constituents of this howler, new notices were being printed up!

"An honest observer," Mrs. Robinson remarked in 1981, "including a sitting senator, must conclude that the Senate is an underdeveloped and underused body which fails to give value for money". That same year the Trinity senator made her second attempt to move from the Upper to the Lower House of Parliament so that she might enter the mainstream of political life.

Even as a senator who was outside the mainstream of Dáil Éireann, her legislative record, during her first period as Labour senator, was impressive.

In this period, two Private Member's Bills engaged a great deal of her time in the House. Disappointed and annoyed with the on-going failure of the Government to introduce a legislative initiative on family planning, she introduced the Family Planning Bill (1978). She was supported by Senators Justin Keating and Jack Harte and it got its First Reading in November 1978. The Government successfully blocked all attempts for further debate on its provisions and, as mentioned earlier, the Irish solution to an Irish problem came into being.

The second Private Member's Bill was the Domicile Bill (1980). The aim of the measure was to abolish the dependent domicile of married women and to lower the age by which they could acquire an independent domicile from 21 to 16 years. The Bill had the backing of the Council for the Status of Women and other women's groups. Mary Robinson saw the measure as having a particular urgency because the lack of independent domicile of women under Irish law prevented Ireland from signing and ratifying the Copenhagen Convention on the elimination of discrimination against women. That agreement had been concluded in July 1980. Mrs. Robinson introduced her Private

Member's Bill on 19 November of that year but, yet again, she failed to get adequate time from the Government for effective debate on the matter.

Few on either side of the House would doubt the effective way in which Mary Robinson used the device of the Private Member's Motion and the Adjournment Debate to raise issues of interest to her. Among those issues raised by way of motion were the following:

In April 1978 she tabled a motion calling on the Government to establish a system of family courts and to introduce a comprehensive scheme of free civil legal aid in Ireland. The Government did not welcome what it saw as her interference in the matter, as it had its own plans in this area. Mrs. Robinson was not impressed with those plans and said so in the House. She introduced a second motion in June 1979 calling for legislation setting out clear policy lines as outlined in the Pringle Report.

In April 1980 she moved a motion on mental illness and people who appear before the courts on criminal charges suffering from same. As usual the Government had its own plans in the area, especially after the publication of the Report on the care of people suffering from mental disorders.

After the publication of the Brandt Commission Report on Third World Aid, Senator Robinson moved a motion calling for an examination of its implications for Ireland's contribution to development policy. During the course of the debate the Minister for Foreign Affairs, Brian Lenihan, restated Ireland's commitment to reaching the UN target of 0.7 per cent of GNP by the end of the '80s.

Mrs. Robinson was pleased to have that commitment restated as there had been some fears that the Government might renege on it.

Mary Robinson was Chairman of the Social Affairs Sub-Committee of the Oireachtas Joint Committee on EEC legislation and she moved several motions on its affairs in the Senate. She gave a public airing to EEC-related matters that might otherwise have been lost in the pages of officialdom. Such motions were widely reported in the national media and did much to consolidate her image as the sacred keeper of social legislation in Ireland.

Raising Motions on the Adjournment in the Senate is made difficult by the restrictive procedural requirements governing them. The Trinity senator made very effective use of this parliamentary tactic, and it often allowed her to debate on the record of the House, and in front of the responsible Government Minister, matters of interest to her.

On three separate occasions she used this device of the Motion on the Adjournment to highlight inadequacies in the social welfare system. Most notable was when she brought the then Health Minister, Charles Haughey, into the Senate chamber for an Adjournment debate on the possibility of using Section 17 of the Social Welfare (Supplementary Allowances) Act 1975 to improve the position of deserted wives, by involving the Health Boards in paying the allowance immediately in the first instance, and subsequently taking legal proceedings against any husband in a position to maintain his wife.

The Senate Debates for this period also show that Mary Robinson played a very active part in examining Government Bills, often drawing attention to possible pitfalls in the proposed legislation.

When a general election was called for 11 June 1981 Mary Robinson - with the confidence of someone who had polled well at the last general election, been elected to Dublin City Council in 1979 and performed impressively in the Senate - sought a Labour Party nomination in Dublin West. She set about attempting, with renewed vigour, to fulfil her long-standing ambition to be a Dáil deputy. As she faced this next hurdle of her political career, Mary Robinson hoped that the internecine strife which beset the Labour Party campaign in Rathmines West would be avoided on the battlefield of her new constituency.

14

THE LAST HURRAH: DUBLIN WEST

James Joyce could quite easily have been the architect of the constituency of Dublin West - it contained, after all, part of the hinterland of Finnegans Wake - Chapelizod. It contained much more. Few Dublin constituencies had as diverse a collection of electors than that held within its boundaries. Its voters lived in such unconnected parts of the city as Cabra and Castleknock. The river Liffey flowed right through it, and, at its lower extremity, the Grand Canal provided a natural boundary.

As constituted for the 1981 general election, Dublin West was part city and part county. It had pockets of isolated middle-class wealth in suburban Lucan and Castleknock; well-heeled farmers in Porterstown and Clonsilla; working-class poverty in the run-down corporation estates of Ballyfermot. It was in some respects, at least, early '80s Dublin in microcosm. It held the sprawling new housing estates of Blanchardstown and Mulhuddard and the old settled inner city communities of Mount Brown and Kilmainham. It was on this disparate ground that Mary Robinson made her last stand for Dáil Éireann. It was also on this ground that she made her first electoral stand against Brian Lenihan. In practical political terms this five-seater constituency was what has now entered the language of political commentary as a "key marginal".

There were 15 candidates seeking the five seats, and at least six of them were national personalities with high public profiles. The mistaken opinion, across party lines in the constituency, was that Brian Lenihan would lose his seat. The more accurate prediction was that

Jim Mitchell of Fine Gael would top the poll; that Tomás MacGiolla of Sinn Féin the Workers' Party would fail to take a Dáil seat and that the way in which this constituency voted would forecast the shape of the new Dáil.

Fine Gael also fielded Dick Burke, the former Education Minister and European Commissioner, along with Brian Fleming, a member of Dublin County Council and a vocational teacher.

One of the earliest features of the campaign was a split in the Fine Gael camp. At one point the Party's national executive intervened to prevent Dick Burke from withdrawing his candidacy. Literature canvassing support for Brian Fleming, which contained not so much as a mention of the other Fine Gael candidates, was circulated in Dublin West. The Fine Gael election strategy committee demanded that it be withdrawn. The committee also gave instructions that Mr. Fleming's canvassers must canvass on the whole Party ticket and not just on his behalf.

The Fianna Fáil ticket included, along with Brian Lenihan, Eileen Lemass, who had first taken a seat in 1977 in the Dublin Ballyfermot constituency, Liam Lawlor who was dogged by a land speculation controversy, and Councillor Tommy Boland.

It came as a considerable relief to Mary Robinson's campaign staff that, this time out, Labour's internal wrangling was not the focus of media attention. She could also rest safe in the knowledge that she had the active support of Labour Senator Jack Harte. In a constituency with such large working-class pockets his support was a particular bonus. Jack Harte's upbringing was straight out of the pages of Seán O'Casey. His early years were spent in a tenement in Dublin's Little Denmark Street. His mother's family were supporters of James Larkin. At the age of twelve Jack Harte had left school to become a delivery boy. He was a member of the Administrative Council of the Labour Party for many years. Such a man was a useful asset to an upper middle-class girl from Ballina as she negotiated the rougher spots in Dublin West.

Mary Robinson was Labour's front runner and the only candidate of three who had a chance of taking a seat for the party. The others were Anne McStay and Eamon Tuffy. Mrs. McStay, a housewife from Ballyfermot, was a well-known spokeswoman on women's issues. She had been a Labour candidate in the Ballyfermot area in the 1979 local elections. Eamon Tuffy, a physics lecturer, lived in Lucan and was the chairman of the local branch of the Labour Party.

The team was competing for votes that might be expected to go to candidates like Tomás MacGiolla or Michael Finegan of SFWP. Those candidates were thought to have broad appeal in the working-class areas of Dublin West. Mary Robinson was expected to appeal to the middle-class voters. What could not be expected of her was that she would win the large personal vote left behind by Labour rebel Dr. John O'Connell in Ballyfermot, after he moved his base to Dublin South Central. Nor could she be expected to do exceptionally well in the broad sweep of the working-class areas of Dublin West.

She faced into the campaign with confidence.

"I have come in as a new candidate," she told Renagh Holohan in *The Irish Times*, "and what is most important is that we have a very united and cohesive campaign... I would be very depressed if Labour can't take a seat in a major urban community."

All candidates agreed that the two major problems facing their potential constituents were unemployment and prices.

Mrs. Robinson campaigned on those two issues and on the Labour Party's plan to re-introduce the wealth tax and increase some taxes while subsidising basic foodstuffs. She also campaigned on local bread and butter issues, like the Regional Technical College for Blanchardstown, bus lanes to improve public transport, the provision of health and shopping centres in the new housing estates.

In her speeches she pushed home the message of Labour's manifesto - its first in 12 years. The document stated that the Irish economy was in a state of crisis. It proposed a three-year economic and social plan. It detailed a wealth tax and a comprehensive capital taxation system. There was no mention of nationalising the banks but there was mention of removing the prohibition on divorce.

On the North the manifesto said that the Party aspired to the unity of Ireland but said that unity could only come about through reconciliation between the two communities and the creation of institutions there, built on power-sharing.

The manifesto received very little media attention and that which it did receive focused on things like the wealth tax and, of course, the Party's position on coalition. Garret FitzGerald said that Fine Gael would be prepared to discuss with Labour the formation of a Government if the need arose. There would be no compromise from Fine Gael on the wealth tax and the programme to be implemented in Government would be Fine Gael's.

All this talk of coalition brought out some of the anti-Labour hysteria that characterised the 1969 general election. In Kerry, Tom McEllistrim of Fianna Fáil was quoted as telling the farmers of the county:

"Vote for a coalition and they will move in and take over your land."

During the campaign the *Longford News* quoted Albert Reynolds, then Minister for Communications, as saying, "the Labour Party seek to bring in divorce and abortion which is totally against the wishes and values of the Irish people. Abortion is murder and the people want no part in it". Those people in the Labour Party - and this included Mrs. Robinson - who favoured a referendum on the constitutional ban on divorce were described by Minister of State Seán Doherty, in the same newspaper, as "attempting to impose by stealth a view of society not shared by the majority of our people". One Fianna Fáil councillor went so far as to say that a vote for Labour was not a vote for marriage, but a vote for living in sin!

While Labour was doing battle against such attacks on a national level, Mary Robinson was having her own problems with a well orchestrated smear campaign in Dublin West.

Residents in the better-heeled suburbs of the constituency took grave exception to the large number of travelling families parked on their doorsteps. It was alleged by Opposition canvassers on those very doorsteps, that Mrs. Robinson had obtained a court injunction to prevent the travellers from being moved on. She countered with a letter on Senate notepaper dated 3 June 1981. It said the allegation was the work of a "dirty tricks brigade".

She explained to the voters how it would have been impossible for her to obtain such an injunction because she was having a baby and fighting the election campaign, and that had kept her away from the courts for several months.

As Mary Robinson delivered the Labour Party gospel in the constituency, she was well received on the doorsteps right across its not inconsiderable social divide. By 1981 she was one of the best-known women in Ireland. As in the 1977 campaign in Rathmines West, some of her canvassers recall that her apparent inability to make small-talk coupled with a natural shyness with strangers, made her appear rather formal and stiff. Helping to dispel that image was the presence of her newly-born son Aubrey, whom she was breast feeding in what an election worker termed "safe houses" in the constituency.

Labour and Fianna Fáil were concerned about a nationwide factor which was new to recent Irish general elections. The cause of that concern was the H-Block candidates who were contesting the election to highlight conditions in the Maze Prison in Northern Ireland. When the campaign began some of the H-Block candidates were on hunger strike in support of their demands. Republican feeling was at an all time high in the border constituencies and there were reports at the time that Labour members in Dundalk had left the Party to canvass for the H-Block candidate there.

Dublin West had its H-Block candidate, Tony O'Hara, who was a prisoner in Long Kesh. He was a member of the IRSP and his brother, Patsy O'Hara, was one of the best-known of the Maze hunger strikers. Fianna Fáil feared that his candidature would seriously hinder its chances of taking a third seat. Labour was concerned that he would take votes that might otherwise fall their way. Mary Robinson's supporters felt that there was little chance that the type of voter who would give her a number one vote would be switching allegiance to a H-Block candidate. In the end Dublin West did not elect a H-Block candidate but he polled a higher percentage of first preference votes than Mrs. Robinson. Two of the H-Block candidates, Paddy Agnew and Kieran Doherty, were returned to Dáil Éireann. One died on hunger strike some weeks after the election, and the other was hardly in a position to take up his seat.

The overall result of the election was bad news for Labour. The result in Dublin West was particularly bad news for Mary Robinson. Her poor showing put an end to her aspirations for election to the Dáil.

The quota was 7,794 votes. There was a voter turn out of just over 70 per cent which the Robinson camp felt would help their candidate.

On the first count preference table she was in ninth place, polling only 2,342 votes, just 664 more than Tomás MacGiolla of Sinn Féin the Workers' Party. Jim Mitchell of Fine Gael headed the poll, as expected, with an impressive 9,326 first preference votes.

Mary Robinson held out until the eleventh of twelve counts. Interestingly, of the remaining candidates on that eleventh count - Fleming, Burke, Lemass and Lawlor - she received the highest percentage of transfers after the elimination of Tony O'Hara the H-Block candidate. But her final result of 4,832 was far short of the quota. The twelfth and final count saw Dick Burke and Brian Fleming of Fine Gael and Fianna Fáil's Eileen Lemass returned to Leinster House.

Mrs. Robinson's failure to make the impact expected of her by Labour, and the loss of the seat held by Liam Lawlor were the most interesting aspects of the result from Dublin West. Curiously the wrangling between Dick Burke and Brian Fleming helped rather than hindered the Fine Gael vote.

The level of Mrs. Robinson's disappointment could be gauged from a remark she made in an interview with the *Irish Press* just after the election. She said she had discovered a lack of political consciousness among working-class people. They did not respond, she said, "with any degree of political awareness of their critical position and seemed to have no perception of the degree of social change necessary to alter their predicament".

There were many Labour politicians who shared this view with Mary Robinson, but none was so bold as to give it public airing, with the exception of one Labour politician who said on RTE television that the Dublin working class should be "examining its conscience" for having failed to elect Frank Cluskey.

In the election, Labour's share of the vote plummeted to its lowest since 1957. In Dublin the result was particularly disastrous for the Party. It halved its number of seats, taking only three of the forty-eight. Most prominent of the victims was Party leader Frank Cluskey. Within days of the election Michael O'Leary had succeeded him.

Nationally, in terms of seats, Labour dropped from seventeen to fifteen. The Party was divided on why its performance had been so disappointing. The pro-coalition lobby maintained it was because the Party failed to make its position on coalition clear before the election. The anti-coalition lobby were of the view that the Party would have fared better if it had ruled out coalition altogether.

Overall, Fine Gael made substantial gains, winning a higher share of the vote than ever before. Fianna Fáil's drop in popularity was expected. The economy had gone through yet another bad patch and the Party could hardly have expected to maintain the unusually high share of the vote it had won in 1977. For Labour the thorny question of coalition with Fine Gael again raised its unwelcome head.

Mary Robinson was opposed to coalition. She made her position quite clear in a letter to her new Party leader, Michael O'Leary. "There is no place for a coalition deal with Fine Gael in that process of recovery and strengthening of the Labour Party," she wrote, in a letter also signed by Councillor Pat Carroll. Like Mary Robinson, he too had failed to take a seat for the Party in Dublin.

The letter said that they were both concerned that any negotiations which Mr. O'Leary had with Fine Gael should be set in the broader context of the long-term interests of the Party and the Labour

131

movement.

She favoured talks with independent deputies on the Left so that an *ad hoc* strategy could be drawn up for the support of a minority Government, which would be obliged to adapt its policies to the priorities of the Left if it wished to continue in office.

Mrs. Robinson's letter to Michael O'Leary said that any price is too high for entering a coalition with Fine Gael because of the damage it would do to Labour's identity and to "its central purpose of pursuing socialist objectives".

Michael O'Leary's own constituency of Dublin Central voted against coalition but 60 percent of the Party members who attended a Labour special delegate conference on the coalition question endorsed a coalition deal with Fine Gael.

When the 22nd Dáil convened on 30 June 1981, Fine Gael leader Garret FitzGerald was elected Taoiseach by 81 votes to 78. Michael O'Leary became Tánaiste in the new administration. The outgoing Fianna Fáil Government had been in office since 5 July 1977. It would be on the Opposition benches a mere seven months.

Meanwhile,Mary Robinson was without a seat in parliament. To rectify that position she appealed once again to the electors of her old university.

15

THE MORAL CIVIL WAR

Mary Robinson's failure to secure a Dáil seat in Dublin West marked a watershed in her career as a public woman. While hope springs eternal, deep in the consciousness of many an aspirant to a Dáil seat, this was not the case with Mrs. Robinson. Soon after her defeat she remarked how politics in Ireland was very much a full-time job. She was aware that if she were to secure a seat in Dáil Éireann it would be at the cost of her academic and legal career, and while she continued to be deeply immersed in those twin careers, a Dáil seat would most likely elude her. After several Senate and two general elections, Mrs. Robinson was as hard-nosed and practical a grassroots operator as any to be found in the usual habitats of that political animal.

Mrs. Robinson sat to write the usual finely constructed manifesto to the electors of Dublin University. This one dwelt at somewhat greater length on her legislative record, but in its opening section she referred to her recent defeat in the general election:

"I now present myself for re-election at a time of one of the worst economic crises this country has faced. High inflation and unemployment are already ravaging the most vulnerable and least resistant sections of the community. The indecisive result in the recent election showed an anxiety in the electorate for immediate solutions to those problems, but great uncertainty as to how they might be resolved. As a member of the Labour Party actively involved on Dublin City Council I am acutely conscious of the inequality in our society and of the suffering of the less well protected. I sought to participate directly as a member of the Dáil in providing a political framework within which to work towards resolving these problems. I did not get that mandate. But I return to this electorate with an even deeper sense of purpose."

She was working up to an important statement on the North, which is significant in the light of the reasons she would later offer for her departure from the Labour Party.

"I continue to believe that the South - with the luxury of greater political stability - has failed to see the importance of developing fully as a pluralist society which accommodates differing moral and social attitudes and which safeguards and protects minorities. In the past four years we have regressed in this regard as evidenced by the hypocrisy underlying the Health (Family Planning) Act 1979 and the refusal by the Government to contemplate even discussion of constitutional change on divorce."

She pushed the message home in plain language:

"Whatever our futures, we are bound together in North and South as witnesses of the tragedy, waste and turmoil of more than a decade. We are bound together also in the severity of the economic and social problems on the ground in both parts of Ireland. Time is not on our side in seeking a political framework within which to make progress."

Then came the passage which made it quite clear that Mary Robinson would be one politician in the Republic for whom the Anglo-Irish Agreement - when it came to be signed - would be an unpalatable instrument:

"I do not believe that framework should be founded on secret negotiations between the Dublin and London Governments which exclude knowledge and participation by the representatives of the communities in Northern Ireland. However, it is essential to maintain a political momentum at the highest level in relation to the North, and to involve Northern representatives directly in any such discussions, because a political vacuum at present would lend encouragement to the advocates of violence in pursuit of their goals."

With those words the campaign to keep Mary Robinson in the

Senate got under way. Ballot papers were sent out to the 9,270 Trinity voters on 10 July.

Senate campaigns are usually low-key affairs from the viewpoint of the general public. For the candidates, they are anything but. In the 1981 campaign 130 candidates sought 43 seats on the Senate panels and 25 graduates sought election to the six university seats - the only ones voted on by a non-political electorate. Given the input of local councillors into the election of senators, it was a foregone conclusion that Fine Gael would sweep the board in the 1981 election to the Upper House. Their gains in the 1979 local elections guaranteed that. Added to that advantage was, of course, Garret FitzGerald's right as Taoiseach to nominate his own eleven senators.

When Mary Robinson confirmed her intention to seek re-election to the Senate on the Trinity panel, she told *The Irish Times* that due to the tight voting situation in the Dáil, the Senate would be of more crucial political importance than ever. She correctly predicted more of a party political interest in the six university seats this time out.

Mrs. Robinson was criticised by Kieran Mulvey of the Association of Secondary Teachers of Ireland when he announced the ASTI's officially endorsed candidate, Kevin Meehan. "I think it is reprehensible of people like Mary Robinson, Gemma Hussey and John Horgan to use the university seats as a resting ground, after they have been rejected by the electorate," Mr. Mulvey told Christina Murphy of *The Irish Times*. Mrs. Robinson had no difficulty with her party political status. She had already pointed this out to the Trinity electorate last time out, and she now pointed out the fact that after the last Senate election Dr. Conor Cruise O'Brien and herself had been returned for Trinity.

Gemma Hussey of Fine Gael took basically the same stand. "My party political affiliation has not impeded in any way my freedom to speak on all issues and I intend, if elected, to carry on in exactly the same way," Gemma Hussey told *The Irish Times*.

Amongst the other candidates for the Trinity seats were: Trevor West - Mrs. Robinson's first election agent; Catherine McGuinness,

135

who had taken a Senate seat in the by-election caused by the resignation of Conor Cruise O'Brien in 1979; Shane Ross, who had run against Mrs. McGuinness in that by-election; Dr. David Cabot, the conservationist; David Norris, an internationally-known Joycean scholar and campaigner for the reform of Ireland's draconian laws on homosexuality; Barry Cullen, a social worker; and William Abbey of the Holy Cross Fitzsimon, a retired customs' official who won 236 votes in Dublin South East in the 1981 general election and was also a candidate on the NUI panel.

As an outgoing senator, Mary Robinson had the natural advantage of incumbency, though that in itself guaranteed nothing. The word on the ground was that stockbroker Shane Ross, who had made quite an impression with his postal campaign especially with his strong views on Northern Ireland, could take Mrs. McGuinness's or even Mrs. Robinson's seat. Mary Robinson had defeated his father, John Ross, in 1969.

As it turned out, Shane Ross was elected at the expense of an outgoing senator, but the loser was Trevor West. Ross headed the poll with 1,415 first preference votes, a mere 21 short of the quota. He was elected on the fourth count and Mary Robinson and Catherine McGuinness on the sixth and final count, Mrs. McGuinness without reaching the quota.

Fine Gael emerged as the largest single party in the new Senate; but Fianna Fáil, despite its loss of seats by small margins, performed remarkably well given its weakened voting power at Oireachtas and local council level.

The Senate which was elected in 1981 was a short-lived assembly. The political instability which followed the election of that year saw a change of administration after another general election on 18 February 1982. It brought Fianna Fáil back to power and when the 23rd Dáil assembled on the 9 March, Charles Haughey was elected Taoiseach. His administration lasted until November of that year when a Fine Gael-Labour Coalition assumed power, with Garret FitzGerald as Taoiseach and Dick Spring as Tánaiste. The Coalition had published a 30-page programme for Government which devoted a mere three paragraphs to what was euphemistically called "social reforms".

Mary Robinson was one of a number of Labour Parliamentary Party members who would have wished for a somewhat wider canvas on which to paint the outline of the social and moral issues of her crusade for a pluralist society. Two of those issues dominated her last years in the Senate. They were divorce and abortion - the latter giving rise to what journalist Gene Kerrigan called "the moral civil war".

One of the most colourful battlecries raised in that war originated in Co. Kerry. It came from a Dominican priest, at a mass celebrated in the county in the presence of the papal nuncio, Dr. Gaetano Alibrandi. He invoked the routing of the Turks by the Christians at the Battle of Lepanto in 1571 to rally Catholic Ireland to rise up and vote at the referendum on the Pro-Life Amendment. Voting was scheduled for 7 September 1983. The bitterness which surrounded the campaign was summed up by Labour leader Dick Spring when he observed: "Neighbour has turned against neighbour; eminent professional men have bitterly denounced each other in public; the Churches could hardly be further apart; colleagues in the same political party have launched personal attacks on each other."

In *The Crozier and the Dáil*, John Cooney points out that the idea that a constitutional amendment would be required to prevent abortion being made legal by the courts was first mooted by Father Maurice Dooley, a moral theologian, in a 1974 article in the journal *Social Studies*. The same question came up at a conference on medical ethics in Trinity College, Dublin in September 1980. This led to the formation, the following year, of the Pro-Life Amendment Campaign (PLAC). A right-wing Catholic group, it had phenomenal success in pushing forward the case for a constitutional guarantee for the right to life of the unborn. There were three general elections in 18 months and PLAC therefore had no difficulty in eliciting promises from the politicians.

Fine Gael responded positively when PLAC pointed out that there was a danger of the Supreme Court permitting abortion against the wishes of the Dáil. The party gave a firm commitment in its manifesto for the election of June 1981: "Fine Gael is unalterably opposed to the legalisation of abortion and in Government will initiate a referendum to guarantee the right to life of the unborn child."

Fianna Fáil was more circumspect when Charles Haughey first met with the PLAC supporters. However, he later gave "a solemn assurance" that Fianna Fáil would introduce an amendment if returned to office. Labour gave no specific commitment to PLAC.

In June 1981 Dr. FitzGerald was back at the helm of Government and he assured PLAC that the Attorney General, Peter Sutherland, was at work on a wording for the amendment but it was a difficult process. When Dr. FitzGerald's administration collapsed in January 1982 PLAC re-mounted its campaign. Mr. Haughey said he would enact the amendment in 1982 while Dr. FitzGerald promised there would be a referendum during the lifetime of the next Dáil. Fianna Fáil was returned to power in March and during the last days of Mr. Haughey's administration Dr. Michael Woods introduced the following wording:

"The State acknowledges the right to life of the unborn and, with due regard to the equal right to life of the mother, guarantees in its laws to respect, and as far as is practicable, by its laws to defend and vindicate that right."

Fine Gael and Labour, in their new joint programme gave this undertaking: "Legislation will be introduced to have adopted by 31 March 1983, the pro-life amendment published by the outgoing Government, which had the backing of the two largest parties in the Dáil. The Parliamentary Labour Party reserves the right to a free vote on this issue."

The Minister for Justice, Michael Noonan, announced that the Government would consider changes in the wording of the amendment, provided they retained the underlying principle that the practice of abortion should not be permitted to creep into Irish law. Mr. Noonan pointed out that advice had shown that on one interpretation, the amendment could positively facilitate the introduction of abortion on a wide scale.

Michael Woods defended his party's wording and said it had taken account of Protestant thinking on the subject. The Protestant Churches, however, did not share his view. On RTE radio, the Church of Ireland Primate, Dr. John Armstrong, went so far as to describe the campaign as reminiscent of the Mother and Child Scheme in so far as the moral theology of one Church was being forced on all the people.

The Attorney General, Mr. Peter Sutherland, advised the Government that, amongst other things, the Fianna Fáil wording left uncertain the life to be protected - that of the mother or the child - thus making it possible for a decision of the courts to legalise abortion.

Fine Gael proposed an alternative wording: "Nothing in this Constitution shall be invoked to invalidate or to deprive of force or effect, any provision of a law on the grounds that it prohibits abortion."

In the Dáil the Fine Gael amendment was defeated by 87 votes to 63. The final stage, with the Fianna Fáil wording, was passed by 85 votes to 11. Most of the Fine Gael Party abstained with only Monica Barnes and Alan Shatter voting against.

When the debate opened in the Senate on 4 May - with a series of critical speeches directed against the amendment by members of Fine Gael and Labour - Mary Robinson spent almost two and a half hours arguing against the proposed amendment, the wording of which she said, would give rise to serious legal, medical and social problems. Maeve Kennedy who was reporting the debate for her *Irish Times* "Senate Sketch" thought it a "remarkable performance. It lasted the best part of two and a half hours. And in the end she had virtually emptied the House and worn down one Minister and two junior Ministers".

Mary Robinson argued that the wording was not amenable to authoritative interpretation without litigation. And she said the intervention of the Catholic bishops in the debate was a step backwards. Senator Robinson said that if the Senate abdicated its responsibility to deal properly with the amendment "then the only honest course is to table a motion at the next sitting of the Senate, calling for our abolition".

She read into the record of the House the comments of the Attorney General and the Director of Public Prosecutions; the findings of the Commission on Human Rights; the views of the minority Churches; the statement of Dean Victor Griffin; the views of the Roman Catholic Archbishop of Dublin; the views of a legal expert; the original press release from the pro-amendment campaign.

From the outset of the whole pro-life amendment debate Mary Robinson took a public stand against the amendment for reasons she made clear at numerous public meetings.

They were reasons which led to her being branded as part of a "pro-abortion" lobby.

Her main arguments were that it would be divisive on religious grounds to enshrine in the Constitution the moral viewpoint of one particular denomination which was not shared by others. The amendment would have no practical impact whatsoever in reducing the number of abortions obtained by Irish women each year. And finally, it distracted from the real social, legal and personal problems in this area.

She described the debate on the whole issue as one which "exposed the unreality of the emphasis on constitutional change". It would be more honest, she had told the electors of the Trinity constituency early in 1983, to face up to Ireland's abortion rate, and to set about taking steps to reduce the number of unwanted pregnancies by removing some of the pressures on the women concerned.

The reasons for her opposition to the proposed amendment were set out most clearly in that 1983 election manifesto:

"On first reading, [the] wording may appear simple and attractive, with a clear meaning which the vast majority of people in the country would be happy to support. However, on closer examination it will be seen to be the opposite: so unclear, and so ambiguous on the fundamental issues, as not to be a suitable text to place before the people to vote on in a referendum. This is because the wording could be construed in a narrow sense to prevent termination of pregnancy except where the mother's life was threatened immediately and directly, or in a much broader sense, where 'life of the mother' could be extended to the quality of her physical or mental life, as has happened with similar wordings in other jurisdictions. The basic problem is that the only authoritative interpretation will be that of judges of the Supreme Court in some future litigation."

Dr. Dominic Conway, the Bishop of Elphin, urged that a Yes vote was a vote for God. From the pulpits of Catholic churches around the country a similar message thundered. However, in line with the new theology, the bishops did say that they recognised the right of each individual to vote according to conscience.

The turn-out on voting day was low - 53.67 per cent. The proposed constitutional change was adopted by a two to one majority but with a narrower margin in Dublin than in the rest of the country.

The Labour Party Leader, Dick Spring, said that the campaign represented a back-lash against the slow liberalising of Irish society. And it was in that context too, that Mary Robinson viewed the Eighth Amendment to the Constitution. The passing of the amendment was but one battle in Ireland's on-going moral civil war.

The other constitutional amendment which engaged a great deal of Mary Robinson's attention in the twilight of her Senate career was the proposal to remove the constitutional prohibition on divorce. She had spoken out against the ban on divorce in her first period as senator, and in April 1980 she had drafted a Bill designed to remove the constitutional ban while still being supportive of marriage.

"The constitutional ban must be removed," she told her Trinity constituency, "after which the Oireachtas would be able for the first time to consider what kind of legislation it might envisage and what important safeguards should be included."

The All-Party Committee on the Constitution had made a unanimous recommendation in 1967 that the absolute prohibition on divorce in Article 41.3 of the Constitution be removed. The Committee recommended that a formula be substituted permitting divorce by those whose religious or ethical beliefs permitted it.

In December 1974, during one of her earliest public statements on the divorce debate, Mrs. Robinson considered the Committee's findings at length. She told a meeting of the Irish Association of Civil Liberties, in Dublin's Shelbourne Hotel, that the Committee had commented on the fact that the constitutional provision was more rigid than the position of the Roman Catholic Church, which would grant a nullity in circumstances not recognised by the State, thus leaving a situation where no marriage existed according to the Catholic Church but still existed according to the State.

The Committee included David Andrews, TD, Senator James Dooge, Sean Lemass, TD, Sean Dunne, TD, Robert Molloy, TD, Michael O'Kennedy, TD, T.F. O'Higgins (later Chief Justice), and James Tully, TD. Amongst their findings was that the absolute prohibition on divorce in the Constitution was "a source of embarrassment to those seeking to bring about better relations between North and South, since the majority of the Northern population have divorce rights..."

Despite the findings of the Committee, the Oireachtas was slow to debate the removal of the constitutional prohibition but outside parliament the momentum for change was gathering. Mary Robinson viewed the issue in the broader context of a review of the Constitution, in keeping with her crusade for a pluralist society. In her 1974 speech in the Shelbourne and in a speech made to the Law Society in University College Galway on 1 March 1976, she drew the same conclusion: "The failure to evolve proper humane civil remedies for the sharply increasing evidence of marriage breakdown in Ireland has resulted in legal instability, hardship and injustice. The approach should be a two-fold one; including both extension of the grounds for civil annulment by passing a law to that effect, and also removing the absolute prohibition on divorce, preferably in the context of the enactment of a new Constitution, so that a comprehensive marriage law may be enacted providing for divorce and re-marriage within the State."

The senator found no shortage of people who disagreed with her views. The letters pages of the national newspapers was the obvious forum for this constituency. Mary Kennedy, the Hon. Secretary of the Irish Family League was one of the more indefatigable correspondents. In the letters page of *The Irish Times*, on 2 October 1979, we find her saying that in promoting divorce, contraception and secular education, Mrs. Robinson's objective was not the unity of Ireland but "to change the laws to accord with those of the UK in the areas of sexual morality and the family. And this is slavery".

This form of disapproval was at least less distressing than the hate mail and used condoms which arrived at her office during the contraceptive debate and, at the very least, the letters were signed. Mary Robinson usually replied to the more reasonable letters. Her reply to Mary Kennedy is a good example:

Sir,

Help! How do you bail out of the voluminous correspondence of Ms. Mary Kennedy of the Irish Family League? I have neither the stamina nor the time to respond in detail to the mixture of innuendo, guilt by association and misrepresentation contained in her letter... facing the inevitability of further correspondence along the same lines. My statements I am prepared to stand over and defend; those of Ms. Kennedy relating to me I must leave to the fairness and common sense of your readers.

Yours etc.,
MARY ROBINSON
Seanad Éireann.

Mrs. Robinson was gathering an ever-widening circle of detractors as the divorce debate rattled on.

Garret FitzGerald and Dick Spring promised the establishment of an All-Party Committee of the Oireachtas before the end of 1983, to review the reform of the marriage laws and look at the legislative and constitutional implications involved. The establishment of the

Committee was delayed by the anti-abortion referendum, but when its membership was announced Mary Robinson's name was on the list.

In the *Irish Independent*, Don Buckley reported that "conservative members of the Committee, particularly some of the Fianna Fail representatives, who may not have realised the full extent of marriage breakdown, have had their eyes opened by the flood of submissions when evidence was invited from the public". Nearly 90 per cent of those submitting favoured divorce. The Committee had difficulty in ascertaining the exact extent of marriage breakdown in Ireland. The Divorce Action Group was suggesting a figure of around 70,000 persons including children - a figure stoutly rejected by some members of the Catholic Hierarchy.

Various legislative initiatives were moved before the Dáil, and Senate passed the enabling Bill for a referendum seeking the removal of the constitutional ban on divorce. The signal which pointed towards the divorce issue as the next hurdle in Garret FitzGerald's constitutional crusade was given in the Senate on 27 November 1985 when he said: "Towards the end of healing the divisions between nationalists and unionists, I believe that we must tackle our constitutional laws which represent an impediment to the establishment here of a pluralist society upon which basis alone we can credibly propose to Northern Unionists in time a coming together in peace and by agreement and free consent of the two parts of Ireland."

While it signalled the onward march of a crusade that Dr. FitzGerald had outlined in an article in *Studies* in 1964 and reiterated many times thereafter; it also signalled the drawing of battle-lines for yet another conflict between Church and State.

Mary Robinson took to the public platforms around the country.

"The referendum of June 26th will be a watershed for the country; a turning point in our national life," she told a Divorce Action Group meeting in Coolmine Community School in early June 1986. She disagreed with the view of the Minister for Foreign Affairs, Peter Barry, that a defeat in the referendum would not have any bearing on North-South relations. "On the contrary," she told that Coolmine audience, "if a majority of people in the South were to say no in this referendum it would have the effect predicted by W.B. Yeats in 1925, it would 'put a wedge into the midst of this nation'. Northern eyes are watching very closely the way this debate is developing."

Mrs. Robinson was fond of invoking the shade of W.B. Yeats, especially on the divorce debate circuit. While the line about putting a wedge into the midst of the nation is a fine touch for an orator to invoke, it does not take account of the fact that Yeats's speech on divorce was argued on aggressively sectarian lines, and it caused considerable offence in Ireland at the time.

However, it was evident from many of her speeches on divorce that Mrs. Robinson herself was monitoring Northern opinion, of all religious shades, quite closely.

She also made a close study of Northern Ireland's divorce laws in the belief that it was helpful in explaining to people in the South the type of reasonable and well-structured legislation which she wished to see in place.

The two diverse strands of Northern opinion were well known in the South and could be represented by remarks of John Hume and Ian Paisley.

John Hume of the SDLP was in Dublin to address the Association of European Journalists on Friday 6 December 1985. At the meeting in Elm Park Golf Club he was asked if the Republic should introduce divorce to please the Unionists in Northern Ireland. He replied that "the South should not be changed to please the North, but should introduce change on its own merits".

The Rev. Ian Paisley was already on record in relation to various aspects of constitutional change in the Republic. He saw such proposals as doing little to alter what he called "the Roman Catholic theology which underlines the 1937 Constitution".

Cardinal Tomás Ó Fiaich made it known, before the referendum, that the bishops would not be deflected from their opposition to divorce because the Protestants accepted a form of divorce. Nor did he hold with the view that the introduction of divorce in the Republic would help ease relations with Northern Unionists or foster a better climate in which to develop the Anglo-Irish Agreement. "Protest leaders have made it clear on several occasions - on contraception, on divorce and on moral issues - that no change will influence their political outlook," the Cardinal told reporters after a meeting with the Taoiseach, Dr. FitzGerald, on 7 April 1986 - just two weeks before the Government announced its intentions with regard to marriage, separation and divorce.

A statement issued by the Catholic bishops - just three days after the Government issued the statement on its intentions - made it quite clear that the bishops were not about to stand idly by as divorce was introduced.

Mary Robinson took issue with them over the grounds which they put forward in their statement for their particular stand.

"The bishops' statement is concerned about the effect which the removal of the ban on divorce would have on the definition of marriage," she told a Divorce Action Group meeting in Malahide in the run-up to the referendum.

While she said she recognised both the right and the responsibility of the bishops to speak out on an issue of public concern in which they had a clear interest, she said the focus of their statement was restricted to a narrow framework which failed to address the relevant issues such as the serious implications of marriage breakdown for those involved; the increasing evidence of stable second relationships; and the anomalies created by bigamous marriages and unrecognised foreign divorce.

She charged the bishops with aiming the thrust of their statement towards the view that unless Catholic teaching is enshrined in the Constitution, marriage itself would be undermined.

She also pointed out that at the New Ireland Forum, the representatives of the bishops said they would champion the civil liberties of Protestants in Northern Ireland in the context of any proposal for constitutional change.

She was recalling Dr. Edward Daly's remark to the Forum: "We have not sought, and we do not seek, a Catholic State for a Catholic people."

How, she now asked on the eve of the referendum, could this be reconciled with blocking the introduction of similar civil rights in the South?

Mrs. Robinson said that the result of the divorce referendum would indicate what kind of society existed in the South. She said it would have profound consequences on Irish society and on the attitude of the young towards that society. The outcome of the referendum, she said, would indicate Ireland's willingness to protect civil rights and liberties.

Her position on the divorce question had remained constant for over a decade as she reminded the Senate on 15 June 1983:

"I affirm - as I have done for more than a decade - my own commitment to seeing the ban on divorce removed and our law reflecting the reality and helping people who are caught in a very difficult situation of marital breakdown for whom it is the appropriate remedy in their circumstances, and for the many stable couples in second relationships, or possibly in a third relationship, who are unable to regularise their relationships."

Of the 1,482,644 people who voted in the referendum, 538,279 said Yes to removing the constitutional prohibition on divorce and 935,843 said No.

"The absence of divorce places us in the unique position where we must devise structures and processes for couples involved in marriage breakdown..." What remained of her Senate career she now applied to just such matters.

Those years in the run-up to the 1987 general election proved to be amongst her most productive in the Senate. By that stage she was one of the most accomplished parliamentarians in Ireland, equipped with an understanding of parliamentary procedure that few could rival. She applied that across a wide spectrum.

Two Oireachtas Joint Committees took up a great deal of her time. Her input into the Committee on EEC legislation was particularly valuable for her chairmanship of its Social Affairs Sub-Committee for which she prepared eight key reports, including those on Community Employment Policy, Stock Exchange Regulations, Air Pollution and Equality of Opportunity. The other Committee was, as we have seen, the Committee on Marriage Breakdown.

The Senate Debates show that she spoke on a wide range of Government and Private Member's business in this period - over 40 separate subjects are listed against her name, many dealing with areas of social policy which she saw as vital to her crusade for a pluralist society.

While it was amongst the most productive of times for her, it was also amongst the most troubled in her political career. Mary Robinson was beginning to have anxious and difficult times with the party she had joined in 1976.

Mary Robinson's grandmother Eleanor Dorothy Macaulay Bourke as Master of Fox Hounds on her hunter Tatler c. 1910 (private collection)

The Bourkes at Enniscrone in 1938. Mary Robinson's grandfather H.C. Bourke (back to camera) her uncle Roddy, her father Aubrey, her uncle Denis, grandmother and Susan (Mrs Paget Bourke)

The former offices of H.C. Bourke's Law firm in Ballina (private collection)

The Bourke family home Victoria House, Victoria Terrace, Ballina (private collection)

Dr Aubrey Bourke, Eleanor Bourke and Sir Paget Bourke at Buckingham Palace in 1957 for Sir Paget's Investiture (private collection)

Pearse Street, Ballina in the 1950s

The calling card of Capt. Paget John Bourke Royal Bodyguard to Queen Victoria.
edged in black like all Palace stationery after the death of Prince Albert
(private collection)

Memorial to Lt. Gen. Oliver Paget
Bourke in St. Michael's Church of
Ireland, Ballina
(Michael O'Sullivan)

Sir Joseph and Lady Sheridan before
leaving for a Buckingham Palace garden
party in 1934
(private collection)

Nairobi 1952, taken just days before the Princess Elizabeth became Queen Elizabeth II. Mary Robinson's uncle Paget Bourke and Mrs. Bourke presented to the Royal couple (private collection)

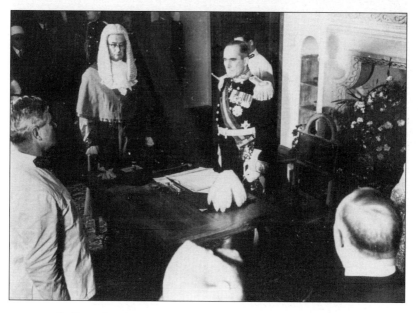

Sir Paget Bourke swears in Sir Hugh Foot as Governor of Cyprus (Crown copyright)

Paget and Susan Bourke in Egypt in the 1940s (private collection)

Sir Paget and Lady Bourke with Archbishop Makarios in Cyprus in the late '50s
(private collection)

Miss Ruddy's School, Ballina (Michael O'Sullivan)

Miss Ruddy's students – Mary with her brothers Oliver, Aubrey, Henry and Adrian (Sunday Tribune)

Mary with her parents and brothers at a Clongowes Open Day, late '50s

Mary at a Trinity Garden Party in the 1960s
(private collection)

Senator Mary T.W. Bourke in 1969 the year of her election to Seanad Éireann (Irish Times)

Nick Robinson, early '70s (Irish Times)

The Senate candidate 1969 (Richard Sealy)

Early days on the public platform (Irish Times)

On the Wood Quay platform with Fr F.X. Martin and Carmencita Hedderman
(Irish Times)

At the Wood Quay site
(Irish Times)

Mary Robinson with fellow TCD academics Kadar Asmal (left) and T.P. McCaughey in the mid '70s (Irish Times)

Mary Robinson with Nobel Peace Prize Winner Seán MacBride

Mary Robinson as Joan of Arc by "Littleman" cartoonist Billy Drake 1978

*Two cartoons by Nicholas Robinson from the Irish Times, Edward Heath (left)
and (right) the lifting of the ban on Catholic attendance at TCD.*

On the Campaign Trail – Above: Rathmines West 1977
Below: Dublin West 1981 with her son Aubrey (Both Irish Times)

Mary Robinson in her Sandford Road home with her dog, Tiger
(Irish Times)

Adjusting the old image, 1990 (Brendan Crowe)

Mary and Nick Robinson (with son Aubrey) voting at the 1990 Presidential Election (Irish Times)

Victory: The President-elect with defeated candidate Brian Lenihan, Taoiseach Charles J. Haughey and Labour Leader Dick Spring

16

TWILIGHT IN THE UPPER HOUSE

Mary Robinson's unease with certain aspects of Coalition policy had begun to manifest itself openly by 1981. In November of that year she threatened, yet again, to vote against the Government in the Senate. The issue was the raising of the school entry age to four-and-a-half years. She had already made her opposition to the proposal known at a Labour Parliamentary Party meeting in early August. Her view on the matter was that without Government commitment to funds for pre-school education, the measure would have had the effect of reducing equality of educational opportunity for those from deprived backgrounds. In the absence of such commitment she made it clear that she was quite prepared to vote against the Government in the Upper House. A growing disillusionment was now perceptible.

By the end of 1981, Mrs. Robinson was reassessing her position as a member of the Labour Party and it appeared from newspaper interviews which she gave throughout that year, that she was heading for a major confrontation with the party she had joined in 1976.

"At the moment," she said in May 1985, "I would find it difficult to go out to canvass a group of young people to join the Labour Party. I would have to be defensive and complicated..." She complained openly that the Party was in need of tougher, clearer policies.

Such confrontation on policy matters with its more intellectual members was hardly a new departure for the Irish Labour Party. It had a long tradition of such internal troubles. Mrs. Robinson's own relationship with the Party had been very much cerebral rather than emotional. It merely remained to be seen which issue would lead her down that road of no return taken in the past by members like Noel Browne and John O'Connell.

The year of her greatest discontent was 1984. In that year Dick Spring was determined to have in his giving the post of Attorney General. The post is usually filled on the recommendation of the Taoiseach. In the summer of 1984 Fine Gael decided that the Attorney General, Peter Sutherland, would replace Dick Burke as Ireland's EC Commissioner. With a Fine Gael candidate heading for Europe, Mr. Spring insisted that a Labour nominee should fill the post left vacant by Mr. Sutherland.

Many members of the Bar, not a few members of Fine Gael, and not least she herself, thought the mantle would fall on Mary T.W. Robinson, S.C., M.A. (Dubl.), LL.B.(Dubl.), LL.M.(Harv.), of the King's Inns and Middle Temple Barrister-at-Law, former Reid Professor of Constitutional and Criminal Law, Constitutional and European law expert, etc.

It did not. Mr. Spring selected his close friend and political confidant John Rogers. Mr. Rogers did not have Mrs. Robinson's experience or qualifications, though those who knew him were confident of his considerable ability. Fianna Fáil did not share that confidence, neither did Garret FitzGerald or many members of the Labour Party. Dick Spring's decision to hold out for the appointment of his friend caused a rift between himself and Dr. FitzGerald that took some time to heal.

"To have my Attorney General chosen for me was something that I instinctively resisted..." Dr. FitzGerald recalled in his autobiography. Dr. FitzGerald would have been quite happy to accept the nomination of Mary Robinson as Attorney General. They moved in the same social circles; their families had even holidayed together in the south of France; they both believed in the crusade for a pluralist society.

Mr. Rogers was just 34 and still a junior counsel. He was required to "take silk" - as the call to the Inner Bar is known - before receiving his seal of office from the President. John Kelly, an eminent Professor of Law, had to do the same thing in 1977.

There was an amusing moment during the Dáil debate on Mr. Rogers' appointment when Charles Haughey sarcastically asked the House: "We all know a Mr. John Rogers, junior counsel, but who is John Rogers, senior counsel?" One answer was, of course, that John Rogers, Senior Counsel, like John Rogers, Junior Counsel, was closer to Mr. Spring than Mary Robinson was.

Mr. Haughey was quite scathing in his remarks on the appointment:

"The new Attorney General has never conducted a case in the High Court, still less the Supreme Court... The main qualification of the appointee is that he is a friend and adviser of the leader of the Labour Party."

Not securing the post of Attorney General was one of the most bitter disappointments of Mary Robinson's public career. Her relationship with the Labour Party and with Dick Spring would never be quite the same again.

"I have a break point," she told Maeve Kennedy of *The Irish Times* in 1985. "It's something that's there at the back of my mind all the time. I don't really want to put it in these terms, but I have made it clear to my colleagues. I have paid a high price for my involvement in the Labour Party, in giving up my independence, and I could go back to it."

Within six months of making that remark she did just that. The reason she gave for that volte-face was that she found the Anglo-Irish Agreement an unacceptable instrument. She expanded on that in great detail in newspaper interviews in late November 1985, but it was to her Trinity constituency that she offered the most detailed explanation of her opposition to the Agreement.

Mrs. Robinson was heavily involved in the negotiations which led to the historic signing of the Agreement by Garret FitzGerald and Margaret Thatcher right from the beginning. She had attended the Airlie House conference held near Warrenton, Virginia, in 1984. It served as a forum for those advocating a peaceful solution to the troubles in Northern Ireland. She had watched closely the proceedings

151

of the New Ireland Forum which led to the intergovernmental negotiations and the drafting, and signing in November 1985, of the Anglo-Irish Agreement. Through it the Republic was granted a limited consultative role in the affairs of Northern Ireland, in exchange for the recognition by the Dublin Government of the North's right to choose its own political destiny.

She participated actively in the Forum debates and would later claim that she "attempted to broaden the political approach in the Forum Report". She said she was instrumental in securing the inclusion of the rather vital provision that the parties to the Forum "...remain open to discuss other views which may contribute to political development". After the signing of the Agreement, Mary Robinson joined the Rev. Ian Paisley and others in condemning it as an imposed framework, unacceptable even to Unionist opinion more moderate than that of Dr. Paisley's.

Before going public on the matter Mrs. Robinson outlined her objections to the Agreement in private communications with Labour Party colleagues and at Parliamentary Party meetings. Colleagues recall her saying that her fears were shared by a significant number of non-Unionists in the North and by many in the Republic who were in touch with the situation on the ground in the North.

Notwithstanding her objections and representations, the Labour Party supported the Agreement and Mrs. Robinson made her return to the independent benches. "We've come to the edge of the abyss, and that's the time when minds are concentrated," she told Maire Crowe of the *Irish Press*. The language was unusual for her. Indeed as Ms. Crowe observed, "since she entered the Seanad in 1969 at the age of 25 Senator Robinson has been spare with displays of public emotion". For a woman whose province had always been cold fact, Mrs. Robinson was now speaking in what she herself described as "apocalyptic terms".

This sudden intrusion of so much personality into an issue indicated the depth of her disillusionment. Maire Crowe remarked how the composure that was Mrs. Robinson's understated trademark almost deserted her as she spoke of her reasons for leaving the Labour Party: "Because of the step I've taken I feel a great loneliness. I have tremendous respect and admiration for the people who negotiated this deal; it gives me no joy, no kudos, no satisfaction to resign. I'm only a modest cog in all of this but I would rather fade out of politics totally, than stay silent. I had the option to remain silent."

The joint meeting between Fine Gael and Labour on the Agreement steeled Mary Robinson's resolve not to remain silent. She had questioned the Taoiseach, Dr. FitzGerald, on the Government's fallback position in the event of the Agreement's failure. Her enquiry elicited the reply that no such eventuality had been entertained. She went home to watch RTE's television news report of the meeting to find that the impression was given that there had been unanimous support for the Agreement. She felt that her opposition, together with that of Frank Cluskey and Paddy Harte, was not acknowledged:

"As I watched that," she said later, "not only did I feel that it was not true as a representation of that meeting, but I knew in my heart that I could not endorse it, and stay silent".

She presented her position as one where, if she stayed in the Party while having such reservations, she would not be able to live with herself. Having consulted her husband Nick and spent a "weekend of solid reflection", Mary Robinson drew up her letter of resignation.

Those who supported her, and those who despised her brand of politics, offered a variation on the theme of her resignation. Some saw it as motivated by the failure to be appointed Attorney General; others viewed it as sour grapes because she knew she was now unlikely to win a Dáil seat; a more Machiavellian interpretation had her leaving Labour only to emerge a year or so later in the "more sympathetic homeland" of Fine Gael.

Maire Crowe put that final possibility to her:

"There was nothing of that in my mind," she replied. She said it was quite clear that her prospects of winning a Dáil seat were not great, in fact, she said she was never really sure of how great those prospects were. She denied that she had any intention of joining another party and said that she was considering leaving politics altogether.

She had made this decision, she said, and was determined to stick by it even if her judgement was wrong:

"I won't have damaged anyone - except myself - and I'm entitled to do that..."

There were elements of the Labour Party which were unlikely to mourn the passing of Mary Robinson from the Party ranks. Her imposition on Rathmines West in 1977 had stirred up considerable bitterness - the sort of bitterness that those involved in the world of back-room party politics take with them to the grave.

Not all of her colleagues saw her as a Saint Georgina doing battle with the forces of darkness. Some would have a certain sympathy for the view expressed in the opening paragraph of that *Man Alive* profile referred to in the early part of this book. It described her as "Blueshirt in background, regarded as a fascist sympathiser by left-wing students in her Trinity undergraduate days, anti-nationalist in outlook".

That hard hitting opening was tempered with the conclusion that "Mary Robinson has plenty of time to make mistakes, learn from them and go on to better things. She is cute. She is able to use people and circumstances brilliantly. She has put Mary Robinson on the map. For a 29-year-old that is not bad going. What will her position be ten years from now?"

Eleven years after the publication of that profile Mary Robinson was giving serious consideration to leaving, not just the Labour Party, but public life altogether.

Her exit from national politics was not to happen just then. She offered herself as candidate again to the Trinity electorate at the Senate election of 1987, in what many close to her thought would be her last campaign.

The central focus of her election manifesto was, as it had often been in the past, Northern Ireland. This time she used the space to outline the main factors which prevented her from endorsing the Anglo-Irish Agreement. The reasons were as follows:

(a) The process of negotiation during 1985, while allowing the SDLP to exert a direct influence through the Dublin Government, excluded any involvement on the British side by the Unionist Parties. Not surprisingly, therefore, the Unionist population regarded it as an imposed framework and were hostile from the start. Unlike the Sunningdale negotiations, cross-community support had not been secured.

(b) The Agreement lacked real balance and credibility, because of the failure of the Irish Government to commit itself to incorporating into the Irish Constitution the guarantee given in Article 1 of the Agreement: that there would be no change in the status of Northern Ireland without the consent of the majority. This failure arose from the belief that such a constitutional amendment could not be carried in a referendum. In other words, we were not asked to pay the price of obtaining a role in Northern Ireland, but had we been asked we would not have been prepared to pay it.

(c) Institutionalising the role of the Dublin Government in the North, in the form of the Maryfield secretariat, was likely to inhibit the political parties within Northern Ireland from agreeing on a form of devolved government.

Fifteen months after the signing of the Anglo-Irish Agreement Mary Robinson said she remained deeply concerned at how attitudes towards it were becoming more polarised and more entrenched.

But there were other matters which her Trinity constituency would be concerned with, and she turned to address these, in what was to be her last Senate election manifesto.

That constituency had changed considerably since Mary Robinson first stood for the Senate in 1969. It was no longer dominated by conservative Protestant opinion. The number of graduates entitled to vote had risen from 6,625 in 1969 to 14,737 in 1987. The base of the constituency had been broadened by an agreement reached between Trinity and the City of Dublin Vocational Education Committee whereby TCD would award degrees to the approved courses of member colleges of the Dublin Institute of Technology. Mary

Robinson made a direct appeal for support to those first-time voters. Trinity College itself had also changed. It was no longer the introspective Elizabethan foundation "within the walls", but was very much a part of the new Ireland, or, in Jack Lynch's words, it had "entered the mainstream of Irish life".

Mrs. Robinson reminded the voters that this particular election was being strongly contested, with the three sitting senators - Shane Ross, Catherine McGuinness and Mrs. Robinson herself - seeking re-election, and a number of very strong candidates in the field. Those candidates included David Norris who by 1987 had one of the highest media profiles in Ireland; Ben O'Rafferty a popular Dublin solicitor who had been very active in Fine Gael as an undergraduate, and W.J. (Bill) McCormack a highly respected academic and well known as the poet Hugh Maxton.

Facing into the election, Mary Robinson had good reason to fear that her seat might be in some danger. Shane Ross had made steady inroads into part of her support base, especially in Northern Ireland. David Norris had the advantage of not just a high media profile but the fact that, as a popular and well-respected lecturer in Trinity, he had contact with a large number of the more recent graduates. There was genuine cause for some concern, so Mrs. Robinson appealed directly to the voters: "I would urge you to discount any suggestion that my seat is safe and that your No. 1 could be better employed elsewhere." The concern which Mrs. Robinson and her advisers had for the security of her seat came to light in a rather embarrassing piece of back-room election tactics. An earlier letter of support from Dean Victor Griffin of St. Patrick's Cathedral was appended to the back of Mrs. Robinson's manifesto. It was a fulsome account from the Dean of Mary Robinson's virtues as a candidate:

"The Senate would be a poorer place without her and Trinity would lose a valuable voice. Jonathan Swift would certainly have approved of this 'earnest and dedicated champion of liberty'. Please give her support in the Senate election, she richly deserves it," the Dean wrote.

The inclusion of the letter would have been a harmless enough gesture were it not for the fact that its date had been altered to make it appear that it was written especially for this election campaign. It was not. The Dean had already pledged his support to David Norris - a regular worshipper at St. Patrick's - who was none too pleased at the appearance of the letter.

For this, her last Senate campaign, Mary Robinson appointed a new election agent - a woman who would later play a very central role in her public life. Bride Rosney, a science teacher and vice-principal of Rosmini Community School in Dublin, had become friendly with Mrs. Robinson during the heady days of the campaign to save the archaeological treasures at Wood Quay, where the Dublin civic offices now stand as defiant sentinels to campaigns and court battles. This last Senate campaign of 1987 was to cement a working relationship which would later see Ms. Rosney as a Svengali-like figure, appearing to exert extraordinary influence over the shape and style of the Robinson presidency.

The 1987 general election had brought Fianna Fáil back to power with Charles Haughey heading a minority Government. Mary Robinson said the election had been one of the most crucial since the foundation of the State because of the severity of Ireland's economic problems. In her election manifesto she targeted unemployment for special attention but her analysis was little more than a recital of the statistics of unemployment prior to the election, together with a mention of how tragic this situation was for young graduate talent.

During the election campaign the Progressive Democrats had proposed the abolition of the Senate mainly on the grounds of cost. Now, as she prepared to spend her last two years in the Upper House, Mary Robinson outlined to her constituents the benefits of the institution she had so often been critical of. "Undoubtedly there is room for improvement," she wrote, "in the composition, powers and procedures of the Senate; but ultimately its effectiveness stems from the calibre and commitment of those elected."

The total poll was 8,564; the quota 2,138. Shane Ross, stockbroker and journalist, headed the poll and was elected on the first count.

Just 22 votes separated Mary Robinson and David Norris after that first count. Mrs. Robinson had recieved 2,123 first preferences. They were both elected on the second count.

Catherine McGuinness lost her seat and Mary Robinson lost a close associate in the Senate. This was the sixth time that David Norris had contested the election. He had worked hard against the view that he was a single issue candidate concerned only with gay rights. Mary Robinson represented him in his case which challenged in the courts the discrimination against homosexuals in Irish law. Now he would sit with her on the independent benches of the Senate.

After leaving the Labour Party Mary Robinson took on a great volume of major legal work but continued to attend closely to proceedings in the Senate, especially in her favourite role as legislation watchdog. In March 1988 she tabled a successful amendment to the Adoption (No.2) Bill 1987, which called for the abandonment of the rather embarrassing practice of recording the names and addresses of all adopted children and their adoptive parents in *Iris Oifigiúil.*

In those last years in the Senate she took up the cause of human rights abuses in Tibet. She told the Senate in January 1989 that Ireland had been silent and apparently unconcerned at the international level about the treatment of Tibet since it was invaded by China. The Senate was debating a motion noting the 40th anniversary of the UN Declaration of Human Rights and calling on the Government to support international measures to establish human rights in Tibet.

"...much of what has happened to Tibet should evoke deep chords in the Irish people. The suppression of a whole people, so that their independent religious, cultural and social ethos is denied, and they are subjected to the humiliation of being colonised and indeed planted upon to such an extent that the Tibetan people have become a minority in their own country, should evoke an immediate response from us," she told the House.

Ireland opened diplomatic relations with China in 1979 but had remained silent before and for some time after, on the violation of human rights in Tibet. Mary Robinson was in contact with the Irish pressure group Tibet Support through her friendship with members like Anthony O Brien, a relentless worker for the cause of human rights in Tibet. He would later be instrumental in engineering a meeting in Dublin between President Robinson and the Dalai Lama - a meeting that did not especially please the Government who were under pressure from the Chinese embassy to avoid official contact with the spiritual head of the Tibetan people during his Irish visit.

In February, Mrs. Robinson withdrew a rather strongly worded motion condemning the Chinese Government for its treatment of Tibet. Her reason for doing so was that its defeat might have led to misunderstanding and not be representative of the strongly held views of many members of the House. Her decision followed a very constructive debate in which many senators expressed disappointment with Ireland's attitude to the plight of the Tibetan people.

Mary Robinson's decision not to seek re-election to the Senate was announced on 23 May 1989. She said her commitment to the Irish Centre for European Law, which she and her husband administered at Trinity, made it difficult for her to give full commitment to the Senate. Her decision was made with "enormous reluctance" but she now preferred "whenever an election is called, to make way for other candidates of high quality and commitment to carry on the tradition of the university seat".

Her share of the vote had fluctuated sufficiently in the course of her 20 years in the Senate to give Mary Robinson cause for concern on occasion, but if she had wished to remain on as a representative for Trinity she had every reason to be confident that she would continue to be returned. She was also certain by May 1989 that the Dáil seat she had so very much desired would now be very unlikely to come her way.

She returned full-time to the career that had brought her to national prominence.

The tributes in the Senate were of the usual fulsome kind. The Cathaoirleach, Senator Tras Honan, said that Mrs. Robinson had played an extraordinary role in the passage of legislation through the House and even though she had not always agreed with her views, they had always made an impression on her.

Senator Maurice Manning of Fine Gael said that her decision was regrettable, and that as a reforming politician her conscientious contribution to the public would be missed.

Her fellow Trinity representative, David Norris, praised her legal expertise, and Independent Senator John Robb said she was one of the few Southern politicians who was well known in Northern Ireland.

Senator Nuala Fennell of Fine Gael praised Mrs. Robinson's courage and said she was a woman who never compromised on her principles and was an excellent role model for women who followed her. And so the tributes went on.

Mary Robinson ended her Senate career as she had started it - 20 years earlier - with an act of dissension. On 5 July 1989 there was a major row in the House over the Government's decision to pass two important pieces of legislation - The Building Societies Bill and The Central Bank Bill - in one sitting. Fine Gael and the Independents withdrew from the chamber in protest. Mary Robinson said that she regretted that the Government's decision would deprive her of an opportunity to speak on what she said would probably be her last day in the Senate in 20 years.

Senator Mary Robinson then withdrew from the Senate chamber for the last time, thus bringing down the curtain rather dramatically on the last act of a Senate career already crammed with incident.

17

BARRISTER-AT-LAW

"Lawyers are like actors; they prefer to work on a familiar stage with props that are reliable and well known. Indeed, both professions have a remarkably similar need to feel comfortable in planning their entrances and their exits!"

This view of the lawyer was offered by Mary Robinson to a legal seminar in Strasbourg in October 1987. Her own entrance to the legal profession in the late 1960s was, as we have seen, through the Law School of Trinity College Dublin, Harvard University, the King's Inns and the Western Circuit of the Irish Bar. Her exit was made 22 years later after an exceptionally successful and at times highly controversial career.

In 1968 her association with, and knowledge of the law, was mainly academic. In that year she began to acquire her practical experience when she commenced practice on the Western Circuit, on which her grandfather, Henry Charles Bourke, had been a prominent solicitor. She "devilled" - the term used to describe a barrister's apprenticeship - with an old friend of his, a barrister called John Willie O'Connor. O'Connor, himself a Trinity graduate, had a very successful practice and was one of the most popular barristers on the circuit. One solicitor described him as "a small god on the Western Circuit". He later became a Circuit Court judge.

When she joined the Law Library - the institution in Dublin's Four Courts where the barristers' profession is based - Mary Robinson was one of a mere handful of women barristers in practice in Ireland. As a female barrister in a male preserve, she said she found "absolutely no prejudice" against her. On the contrary, she acknowledged that she found it easier to win briefs from solicitors than many of her male colleagues.

She found life on the Western Circuit a somewhat lonely and dull existence, involving a lot of sitting around in small country hotels and pubs, waiting for cases to be called. She felt, however, that the smallness of the circuit gave her an advantage over starting in Dublin.

Life on circuit had its humorous moments. She recalled, many years later, the occasion when an intense address she was making to an all-male jury turned to farce when the foreman winked at her! That particular set of gentlemen jurors of the West of Ireland had never seen a woman barrister before. It's often stated that Mary Robinson was the first woman to practise on the Western Circuit. She was not. Others had done so before her, including women like Molly Dillon-Leetch, a member of that well-known West of Ireland legal family.

"The curious thing about circuit towns," the former Master of the High Court, the late Patrick Lindsay recalled, "was that one did not get to know many people, apart from the solicitors. The hotels were usually quite near the courthouses and our socialising was usually quite self-contained."

That socialising often centred on boozy circuit dinners in favoured hotels in Co. Mayo circuit towns like Castlebar or Westport . They were the sort of gatherings that a young woman recently graduated from Trinity and Harvard, and who had a naturally reserved disposition, would find not especially congenial.

The life of the circuit barrister held little attraction for Mary Bourke, even though her family's legal and social connections in Co. Mayo and beyond, could have guaranteed her a lucrative living. When she decided to make her career away from that world, it was her old university and its Reid Professorship and Senate representation that came to her rescue.

The Irish Bar, unlike its English equivalent, is not organised on the "chambers" system but on the more club-like arrangement of the

Law Library in Dublin's Four Courts. The Library system lends itself, at least in theory, to a more affable arrangement where the young and inexperienced barrister can avail of the assistance of more experienced colleagues who are close at hand. It's an arrangement that doesn't suit everybody and various arguments have been put forward over the years for the abolition of the Library in favour of chambers.

Some colleagues have suggested that Mary Robinson isolated herself from the fellowship of the Law Library by setting up what effectively amounted to a set of chambers in Merrion Square and other Dublin addresses, and later in her home in Sandford Road. She saw clients and solicitors in those rooms or chambers and they were equipped with the law reports and a legal secretary. Others point out that she also had the advantage of direct access to Trinity's law library and therefore had little need of the services provided in the Four Courts.

It seems an unfair criticism given that most established barristers assemble, quite soon after qualifying, a representative library of the tools of their trade, and it would be only the most junior at the Bar who would not have access to secretarial back-up services. The fact that she chose to see clients outside the somewhat intimidating surroundings of the Four Courts is greatly to her credit. It also provided her with the opportunity of bringing her children to the workplace. A barrister recalls that over the years momentary silences in many a serious consultation were pierced by the shrill cry of a Robinson baby demanding to be fed. That barrister also recalls Ann Lane, Mrs. Robinson's secretary, approaching the impressive-looking safe in that Merrion Square office, only to extract from it, instead of the expected legal documentation, the coffee which formed its only contents.

Within a few years of being called to the Irish Bar, Mary Robinson's opinions on constitutional matters were regularly quoted - sometimes in ponderous editorials - in the national newspapers.

The term "constitutional lawyer" is the one most often used to describe her career. Though the constitutional cases in which she participated were many and varied, such an exclusive label is, strictly speaking, not correct. In the course of her legal career she represented a wide cross-section of persons and views ranging from a man who sought the decriminalisation of homosexual acts, a wife who sought to obtain a judicial separation from her husband, a couple who sought equality of social welfare benefits or the illegitimate child who sought equality of treatment with a child born within marriage.

She devoted a considerable part of her legal career to liberalising what were arguably some of the most reactionary laws on the statute books of any country in the industrialised world. She established a reputation as one of the leading authorities on social welfare law and as one colleague observed, "her contribution in the area of public law has been substantial". As an academic lawyer she made European law her special interest and used it to good advantage for many of her clients.

An overview of Mary Robinson's constitutional cases does not permit a neat packaging into a specific area of Constitutional Law. In the following overview, it must be pointed out that Mrs. Robinson was one of a number of Counsel working on the cases referred to, and was not always the principal Senior on the case. In an appendix to this book, a more complete list of her cases may be found.

A core part of Mary Robinson's work in the constitutional field centred around rights which are classified as personal rights and more specifically unenumerated rights - rights which though not specifically referred to in the Constitution have been held by the courts to exist.

One such right is the right to privacy. This right formed the core of her argument in two important cases. In *Kennedy v Ireland* she successfully argued that the State's tapping of journalists' telephones infringed the right to privacy.

The case concerned two well-known political journalists, Geraldine Kennedy and Bruce Arnold, and Mr. Arnold's wife, Mavis, a freelance journalist. In May 1982 the Minister for Justice issued warrants authorising that their private home telephones be "tapped". Counsel for the plaintiffs, led by Mrs. Robinson, claimed that this constituted an invasion of their constitutional rights. In particular it infringed their personal right to privacy under Article 40.3 of the Constitution.

The defence admitted that the warrants were not issued for any security purposes and that there was absolutely no justification for the "tapping". However, they submitted that while the "tapping" was improper, it was not illegal and didn't interfere with any constitutional rights.

The President of the High Court, Mr. Justice Liam Hamilton, thought the question that had to be determined was "whether the right to privacy includes the right to privacy in respect of telephonic conversations and the right to hold such conversations without deliberate, conscious and unjustified interference with and intrusion thereon by servants of the State, who listened to such conversations, recorded them, transmitted them and made the transcriptions thereof available to other persons".

He was of no doubt that it did. The dignity and freedom of an individual could not exist if communications of a private nature were deliberately interfered with. Hence the plaintiffs' constitutional right to privacy had been interfered with. The judge awarded £20,000 damages to Ms. Kennedy and Mr. Arnold and £10,000 to Mrs. Arnold.

In *Norris v Ireland* Mrs. Robinson's main submission was that certain statutory provisions which had the effect of criminalising homosexual acts were unconstitutional since they failed to defend Mr. Norris's right to privacy. By a three to two majority the Supreme Court rejected this. Her views were later upheld by the European Court of Human Rights. The Dáil has since passed enabling legislation giving effect to this decision and Mrs. Robinson has signed the Bill into law.

Another such right recognised is the right to earn a livelihood. In *Cafolla v The Attorney General*, Mr. Cafolla sought a declaration that parts of the Gaming and Lotteries Act, 1956 were repugnant to the Constitution as they deprived him of his right to earn a livelihood. Mrs. Robinson, acting for the Attorney General, successfully argued that they did not. It was one of the few cases in which she appeared for the State or a representative of the State in a constitutional action against a plaintiff.

In the *State (M) v The Attorney General* the unspecified right at issue was the right to travel. Mrs. Robinson was part of Counsel who sought and were granted acknowledgement that the right to travel out of the country was an unenumerated personal right arising under the Constitution.

The first prosecutor in this case was an unmarried mother who gave birth to a baby girl in October 1977. The second prosecutor, a Nigerian national studying in Ireland, was the father of the child. The couple had no plans to marry but they remained on friendly terms. It was decided that the child should be sent to live with the father's parents in Nigeria until he returned to live there permanently.

The child's mother applied to the Department of Foreign Affairs for a passport for the child. She was refused on the grounds that to grant a passport would involve a breach of the Adoption Act 1952. Section 40 of this Act effectively provided that in the case of an illegitimate child under one year of age, the child could not be removed except with the approval of the mother and even if such approval were given - as it was in this case - the child could not be removed except for the purposes of residing with the mother or a relative of the mother, as defined strictly by the Act.

The prosecutors put forward two main arguments challenging the constitutionality of the 1952 Act. It was the second of these that succeeded in court. Counsel argued that the right to travel out of the country was an unenumerated personal right arising under the Constitution and that sections of the Adoption Act had failed to protect and secure that right.

The then President of the High Court, Mr. Justice Finlay agreed, accepting that such a right flowed from Article 40 though not enumerated.

Another example of Mrs. Robinson's work in this area is the case of *O'Brien v Bórd na Móna* which dealt in part with the right to fair procedures in decision making. Because the Board had not given Mr. O'Brien an adequate hearing regarding his objection, the proposed compulsory acquisition of his land was deemed invalid.

Mrs. Robinson was also involved in a number of landmark

constitutional "tax" cases. The most consequential of them was *Murphy v Ireland* which changed the way married couples were taxed. In April 1970, as Senator Mary Bourke, she made her views known on what she saw as the unfair nature of Ireland's tax laws in their discrimination against women.

"The State ought to encourage people to get married younger," she told a lunch-time service at St. Anne's Church, Dublin, on 9 April 1970. "There is a shortage of women in employment. The Constitution should be read differently because there is not the same climate as there was in the 1930s," she told the gathering.

Of the more well-known constitutional cases in which Mrs. Robinson participated, two such are the *de Burca* case of the mid-'70s and the *Webb* case of the '80s. The former case established that certain provisions of the Juries Act 1927 which discriminated against women in serving on juries was unconstitutional. The decision had a major impact on the composition of juries in Ireland. The latter case concerned the now famous Derrynaflan treasure. In that case Mrs. Robinson helped confirm the State's right to treasure trove.

Issues of public morals and freedom of expression arose in the case of *Irish Family Planning Association v Ryan*, when the Censorship of Publications Board banned the sale of a booklet dealing with the subject of family planning. Mrs. Robinson was part of Counsel which succeeded in having the Board's decision reversed.

In the light of subsequent developments two of Mrs. Robinson's best-known constitutional cases were the abortion information cases of the late '80s - *SPUC v Grogan* and *The Attorney General (SPUC) v Open Door Counselling and Dublin Well Woman Centre Ltd.*

Both cases centred on Article 40.3.3. of the Constitution and the right to life of the unborn.

A constitutional provision, Article 44(2), which deals with discrimination on the grounds of religious profession was the subject matter of *M v An Bórd Uchtala* (The Adoption Board). Here, section 12 (2) of the Adoption Act 1952 was declared unconstitutional because it infringed Article 44(2) s.s.3 of the Constitution which provides "the

State shall not impose any disabilities or make any discrimination on the ground of religious profession, belief or status..."

In *Reynolds v the Attorney General* it was sought to add 18-year-old voters to the Register of Electors pursuant to a constitutional amendment, in time for the 1973 general election. The action was not successful in that regard.

In the area of Social Welfare/Employment law Mrs. Robinson's work is not well known outside the legal profession and the interested parties. Her understanding of social welfare matters and of the technical complexity of the law in this area has received considerable praise from the legal profession in Ireland. This area of her work generated neither a great deal of income nor the sort of interest attached to the constititional cases, but this whole area represents an important element in Mrs. Robinson's legal career.

One of her most important cases in this field is *Hyland v the Minister for Social Welfare*, which ensured equality of social welfare benefits for married couples.

Mr. Patrick Hyland, the applicant, was married with one child and was receiving unemployment assistance. His wife was receiving unemployment benefit. In November 1986, the Minister for Social Welfare brought into operation The Social Welfare (No. 2) Act, 1985. The couple fell within the ambit of s.12(4) of this Act. The result was that Mr. Hyland received a lesser sum of unemployment assistance. The applicant argued that this was wrong because it was due to the fact that he was a married man living with his wife. If he were not married or if his wife did not reside with him he would be entitled to receive a higher rate of unemployment assistance. As a result of s.12(4) the total amount payable to the Hylands was £66.80 per week.

Two hypothetical persons, not married but living together with one child dependent, each in the same position regarding entitlement to unemployment assistance and benefit, were put forward as a comparative case. Mrs. Robinson's side demonstrated that the total amount receivable by them would be £77.88 per week - some £11.18 more than the married Hylands.

The applicants therefore claimed that s.12(4) of the 1985 Act was invalid, having regard to the provisions of the Constitution. Mrs. Robinson claimed that it amounted to a failure by the State to vindicate the institution of marriage under Article 41. s. 3. as it penalised married couples. That Article states:

"The State pledges itself to guard with special care the institution of marriage, on which the family is founded, and to protect it against attack."

The respondents countered with an argument based on "counterbalancing benefits" such as those available under legislation like the Family Home Protection Act, and also a range of benefits and pensions available. But both the High Court and the Supreme Court ruled in favour of Mr. Hyland.

In the area of European Law Mrs. Robinson's cases were varied in their nature. They encompass a wide cross-section of different legal areas.

Mrs. Robinson appeared before the European Court of Human Rights on three principal occasions - *Norris v Ireland* which deals with Irish law on homosexual conduct; *Airey v Ireland* which was responsible for the introduction of Civil Legal Aid in Ireland and *Johnston v Ireland* where Ireland was found to be in breach of Article 8 of the Convention for its law relating to illegitimate children. Here the Court declared that the illegitimate child "should be placed legally and socially in a position akin to that of a legitimate child".

Mrs. Robinson was also involved in a number of Commission decisions, perhaps the most important being one which never required an actual Commission decision, as a friendly settlement was reached. This was *Stoutt v Ireland* which helped spur the introduction of the Status of Children Act 1987. Mrs. Robinson also represented clients before the European Court of Justice. Two prominent social welfare and employment law cases that were referred to the Court for preliminary rulings were *McDermott and Cotter v the Minister for Social Welfare* and *Murphy v An Bórd Telecom*. In the former case both plaintiffs succeeded in receiving backdated unemployment benefits because of the unequal treatment of married women in unemployment benefit matters. In the Murphy case the notion of equal pay for equal work was declared to include situations where a lower wage is paid to workers engaged in work of a higher value.

Arguably, the Norris and the Airey cases were amongst Mrs. Robinson's greatest achievements as a lawyer.

Mrs. Johanna Airey married in 1953 and four children were born of the marriage. Her relationship with her husband deteriorated. He drank excessively, threatened her and at times subjected her to physical violence. In January 1972 Mr. Airey was convicted of assaulting her. Later that year he left the family home. For eight years prior to this Mrs. Airey had tried to conclude a separation agreement, but her husband refused to sign the documents drawn up by her solicitor. She then tried to obtain a divorce *a mensa et thoro* (a court decree of judicial separation), the grounds being the alleged physical and mental cruelty to her and their children.

Mrs. Airey was unable to find a solicitor to act for her. She was not in a position to meet the prohibitive costs of the action and it would have proved exceptionally difficult to recover the costs from Mr. Airey. On 7 July 1977 Mrs. Airey's application was accepted by the Commission and on 9 March 1978 the Commission unanimously held that the failure of the State to ensure the applicant's effective access to court to enable her to obtain a judicial separation amounted to a breach of Article 6(1) of the Convention on Human Rights which reads in part:

"In the determination of his civil rights and obligations or of any criminal charges against him, everyone is entitled to a fair and public hearing within a reasonable time by an independent and impartial tribunal established by law".

On 22 February 1979 Mrs. Robinson put forward a number of submissions on the Airey case among which the following were the most relevant:

—That the total inaccessibility of the remedy of judicial separation in the Irish High Court was a breach of Mrs. Airey's right to access

170

to the civil courts which the Irish Government must secure under Article 6(1) of the Convention on Human Rights.

—That the absence of a modern effective and accessible remedy for marriage breakdown under Irish law was a failure to respect Mrs. Airey's family life under Article 8(1) of the Convention: "Everyone has the right to respect for his private and family life, his home and his correspondence."

The Court first examined Mrs. Airey's case under Article 6(1). One of the main reasons put forward by the Irish Government that no infringement existed was that Mrs. Airey did enjoy access to the High Court since she was free to go before the Court without the assistance of a lawyer. The Court did not share that view. The Government also put forward the argument that the consequences of the case, namely that in all cases concerning the determination of a "civil right" the State would have to provide free legal aid. Again, the Court did not share that view.

The Court concluded by a five to two majority that having regard to all the circumstances Mrs. Airey didn't enjoy an effective right of access to the High Court. There was therefore a breach of Article 6(1).

The Court also held that there had been a breach of Article 8 of the Convention. Mrs. Robinson argued that by not ensuring that there was an accessible legal procedure in family law matters, Ireland had failed to respect Mrs. Airey's family life. The Court agreed.

The success of the Airey case in Strasbourg altered, in a fundamental way, the relationship between Ireland's civil law and the ordinary citizen of limited means. Since the judgment, its social implications have altered the lives of a great number of Irish citizens.

The lives of a great many Irish citizens were also altered by the Norris case.

David Norris, a lecturer in English at Trinity College, Dublin, described himself as "congenitally and irreversibly homosexual in outlook and disposition". In November 1977 he sought a declaration that sections 61 and 62 of the Offences Against the Person Act 1861 as

171

well as section 11 of the Criminal Law Amendment Act 1885 were inconsistent with the provisions of the Constitution and no longer formed part of the law of the State. The legislation did not specifically make homosexuality a crime, but it had the effect of criminalising certain homosexual conduct between male persons.

Counsel for Mr. Norris, including Mrs. Robinson, put forward a very strong and well-argued case. In the High Court Mr. Justice McWilliams dismissed David Norris's claims. The Supreme Court, on appeal, upheld the decision of the High Court in April 1983 by a majority of three to two.

In the course of his judgment, the Chief Justice, Mr. Justice O'Higgins said:

"On the grounds of the Christian nature of our State and on the grounds that the deliberate practice of homosexuality is morally wrong, that it is damaging to the health both of individuals and the public, and finally that it is potentially harmful to the institution of marriage, I can find no inconsistency with the Constitution in the laws which make such conduct criminal."

In a final submission before the Supreme Court, Mrs. Robinson argued that Ireland, having signed the Convention on Human Rights, should regard as more than persuasive precedent, the European Court of Human Rights decision in *Dudgeon v the United Kingdom*. Mr. Dudgeon, who lived in Northern Ireland, had successfully challenged the very provisions which Mr. Norris was seeking to have abolished, the Court holding that they were inconsistent with the Convention.

Again this argument was rejected but Mr. Justice Henchy intuitively paid attention to the Dudgeon decision and noted that "one way or another the impugned provisions seemed doomed to extinction".

Mrs. Robinson argued the case before the European Court of Human Rights and judgment was delivered on 26 October 1988 in favour of Mr. Norris, thus ending an 11-year legal struggle, with the Court satisfied that there had been a breach of Article 8 of the Convention.

Thirteen years before that success an *Irish Times* editorial of 15

December 1975 made the following observation:

"Senator Mary Robinson remarked in a recent lecture that it was a pity women did not have greater recourse to the courts in cases of discrimination. She suggested that unequal social welfare benefits or the discriminatory income-tax practices relating to married women might be successfully challenged on the grounds of incompatibility with the Constitution."

Some commentators have tended to focus on the aspects of Mary Robinson's legal career which furthered the cause of women's equality before the law. Her record in striking down legislation or Ministerial Orders which were to the detriment of women's rights is impressive. Examples of her work in that area are notable throughout her career at the Bar. To focus on that aspect alone would be to do a great injustice to a woman who had such a varied and distinguished legal career. In this area of women's rights Mary Robinson was conscious that the Irish Constitution sets defined limits on the role of women in Irish society. Her position was made clear to the Women's World Conference in July 1987 when she said that a Constitution which both prohibits divorce and equates the right to life of the mother with the right to life of the unborn child sets those defined limits.

She helped to challenge those defined limits by helping women who were prepared to use the courts to challenge the system. Their names have become part of Irish legal history - McGee, de Burca, Airey.

In her twin role as legislator and lawyer she was extremely conscious of the potential and the limitation of the judicial process in the area of law reform, not just on women's issues.

She presented her views on what is sometimes called "legislation by judges" at a law conference in Trinity College Dublin in November 1984. When the law is reformed in this way the approach tends to be "piecemeal", she said, in that the Court can only deal with the particular case which comes before it. The broader consequences of such judgments cannot always be addressed. She pointed out that some Constitutional theorists regard it as a weakness in a national system

173

if there is too much dependence on law reform by judges. She also pointed out that the Irish Supreme Court had asked the Government on a number of occasions to give urgent attention to the introduction of specific legislation and the call had been ignored.

Again and again Mrs. Robinson stressed that the law should be an instrument of social change. "It is a hidden infrastructure which conditions our society and pervades almost every aspect of our lives", she said, just three years before her election to the presidency.

"People have different perceptions of law, but on the whole tend to underestimate its scope and influence," Mary Robinson said.

She herself underestimated neither the law's scope nor its influence in a legal career that spanned over 22 years.

It is difficult to find an exact or definitive guide to how successful a barrister is in court. The reported cases show that Mary Robinson was successful in almost 70 per cent of those she was involved in. The statistic is only significant when viewed in the light of the fact that she was party to some of the most significant cases in the recent history of the Irish State.

She continued to practise at the Irish Bar and also continued her involvement with the European Law Centre at Trinity until asked by the Labour Party in February 1990 to leave the law behind her and face the biggest challenge of her public career.

18

A CANDIDATE WITH A PURPOSE

On 5 January 1990, the post-Christmas political stupor was broken by Labour Party leader, Dick Spring, when in the course of a radio interview he revealed that he was intent on ensuring an election for the next President of Ireland. The incumbent in office, Dr. Patrick Hillery, had been head of state for 14 years and Mr. Spring was adamant that he would not let the post fall into the hands of yet another Fianna Fáil party stalwart.

So determined was he, in fact, that he told the astonished interviewer that he was prepared to run himself if necessary. This announcement was dismissed by most political commentators who felt that he was far too young for the job, and that his youth and vitality would better serve the country in a legislative role, rather than in a position that was felt by most people to be merely a pay-off for good party service. Dick Spring was, in other words, engaging in a certain amount of political kite flying.

Dick Spring, it was thought, had merely intended to initiate a meaningful debate about a constitutional office in Irish public life which he felt was rapidly sliding towards obsolescence. *Sunday Press* political correspondent, Stephen Collins, in his book *Spring and the Labour Story*, says that Spring insists he was determined to stand if the party could not find a suitable candidate.

Having successfully focused people's attention on the Presidency he was left with a second and far more difficult problem: which potential Labour candidate would suitably attract the electorate and boost the Party's profile for the forthcoming local elections and the upcoming general election?

Rather than pick a candidate and then base a campaign around a personality, Dick Spring decided to formulate a campaign strategy, which would in effect become a "job description". It was felt that even if this "job description" did not throw up any previously unconsidered names it would certainly eliminate some people who had crossed his mind already.

Former Attorney General and close friend of Spring's John Rogers was, along with his special advisor Fergus Finlay, given the task of preparing the document. With the "job description" almost complete and no sign of any obvious candidate emerging it took a brain-wave from Denise Rogers, the personal secretary of Ruairí Quinn, to come up with a name that would surprise many. Ms. Rogers (no relation to the former Attorney General) remarked that Mary Robinson fitted nearly all of the criteria: she was young, fit enough to endure what would have to be a strenuous campaign and she was known to be a compassionate yet tenacious individual who had dedicated her life to fighting for the rights of the underdog.

She was, Ms. Rogers thought, quite simply the best candidate they could reasonably hope for.

This idea quickly found its way back to Dick Spring and he wasted no time in dispatching John Rogers to approach Mrs. Robinson. They met in her Sandford Road home on 14 February and it was with some surprise that Mary Robinson read the new document for a working Presidency and realised that John Rogers was not merely looking for her opinion on the document but actually approaching her to be a candidate.

Mary Robinson's surprise was justifiable; while her youth, vitality and commitment to social democracy were well known and respected in the Labour Party, she had, after all, left them in a row over the Anglo-Irish Agreement in 1985. She felt no lingering bitterness towards the Party but she realised that should the candidacy come down to an internal election she would have little chance of defeating any longstanding Labour figure in one of the in-house dog fights that had for so long emasculated the Irish Left.

John Rogers was shrewd enough not to try and patronise Mary Robinson or tell her that her selection would be easy; instead he merely put forward the pros and cons of her entering the fray and left her to make up her own mind. Only time would tell whether her curiosity would solidify into acceptance.

A few days later he got his answer. Mary Robinson contacted him and asked that a meeting be arranged between herself and Dick Spring towards the end of April.

The meeting, again to take place in the Robinson home, was attended by Mary and Nick Robinson, John Rogers, Dick Spring, Fergus Finlay and Bride Rosney. Ms. Rosney was to play a key role in the campaign to come.

Dick Spring told Mary Robinson that while he was fully behind her endorsement as Labour's candidate, the decision remained ultimately with the Administrative Council of the Party, which would, in conjunction with the Parliamentary Party, choose the Party candidate.

They then discussed the need for her to gather as broad a base of support as possible, a kind of rainbow alliance encapsulating the multifarious interests and points of view of a young, rapidly developing country.

Mary Robinson accepted all this as being obvious and necessary, but she baulked at the suggestion that she rejoin the party she had left five years previously. She argued that she would be far more attractive to the diverse groups targeted if she were an independent candidate. Dick Spring agreed that while this was true, her "return to the flock", as it were, would greatly smooth her way through the initial selection process. It seemed an intractable situation with Mrs. Robinson insisting that she would remain independent while Mr. Spring was adamant that renewing her membership was essential for success.

Mrs. Robinson then declined the offer and wished Spring the very best of luck in finding a new candidate. Dick Spring left the house wondering where he was going to find one.

Mary Robinson was surprised when, some time later, Dick Spring came back and relented on the membership question; Robinson was back in the frame as quickly as she had left it.

This left Dick Spring with the problem of how he was going to pacify his own hard left wing of the Party who wanted to nominate Dr. Noel Browne. Dr. Browne, despite his several battles with the Party, was still very much the Party elder to a wide cross-section of the membership.

Those who attended the Parliamentary Party meeting on 4 April were surprised when Dick Spring announced that he was going to propose Mary Robinson for the Party nomination. This surprise turned to outrage when immediately after the meeting he released a statement saying that the Parliamentary Party had officially decided to let Mrs. Robinson's name go before the Administrative Council for official ratification.

Of course, the meeting had produced no such outcome and when a furious Emmet Stagg denounced Dick Spring publicly it seemed as if the Labour leader had acted prematurely and was now going to see the whole affair blow up in his face.

In fact, it was yet another piece of sophisticated political manoeuvring from Mr. Spring. That same day he had telephoned Dr. Browne and told him that Mrs. Robinson was now the official candidate. A disappointed and angry Noel Browne listened to the Labour leader in seething silence and hung up. Dick Spring then sent a message to the leader of the Workers' Party, Proinsias De Rossa, and informed him that while the Parliamentary Party had selected her, "the matter will be formalised at the Administrative Council/Parliamentary Party meeting at the end of the month".

What Dick Spring had failed to take into consideration was Mary Robinson's sense of integrity. She resented being prematurely described by him as the official nominee before it was formally ratified. She was also furious that Dick Spring had pulled virtually the same stunt that had played no small part in her resignation from the Party in 1985. On that occasion he had claimed that the Parliamentary Party unanimously supported the Anglo-Irish Agreement. This exaggerated claim, along with what Mary Robinson felt was the exclusion of the Unionist community had forced her out of Labour's ranks before - would it happen again?

In the end Mary Robinson held her ground but feared that Spring's *faux pas* would alienate her from the already potentially hostile party hard-core. This fear was allayed when Michael D. Higgins, a supporter of Dr. Browne, sent a letter to all Party members stating that Mary Robinson was "a candidate that enjoys the respect and admiration of so many in this country". He appealed for a unified campaign.

This statement from one of the most respected members of the Party reassured Mary Robinson that even if she won she would not be hampered by half-hearted campaign efforts of a grudging section of the Party, as she had been when she stood for the Dáil in 1977 and 1981.

The meeting to decide on the candidate was held on 24 April and she was proposed by Dick Spring and seconded by Niamh Bhreathnach. The vote was emphatically pro-Robinson and she won by a ratio of 3-1. The first battle of the Presidential race was won.

Newspaper reports the following day were not overly excited about the news of Mary Robinson's official entry into the race.

One of the readers of the reports was Eoghan Harris, a producer in RTE who had just left the Workers' Party in a row over policy formulation. In a document entitled *The Necessity For Social Democracy* Harris had urged his Party colleagues to abandon their hard-line Stalinist approach for a more user-friendly form of social democracy. The Party had rejected his entreaties and he had been virtually forced to resign.

Feeling isolated from the mainstream of Irish politics and desperately wanting a vehicle to express his vision of a new Ireland he felt that Mary Robinson would be the perfect complement for his brash but exceptionally clever style of publicity and promotion.

The following day Harris sat down and penned a letter to Mary Robinson. The letter, which arrived out of the blue, was as strong an endorsement of her candidacy as Mary Robinson could wish for.

The Robinsons were somewhat intrigued. Mary Robinson agreed

with the main thrust of the letter which advised her to ignore the traditional Labour vote saying, "Politically you have huge ground to make up. You must secure the Fine Gael vote - which you can't do unless you deal with the Distortion issue (Divorce and Abortion). You need to split the Fianna Fáil vote which you can do by pulling their progressive women voters with a bravura campaign. You need Labour/Dublin 4/Abortion/Rape Crisis/Incest and all that like you need a hole in the head."

The Harris letter basically put in plain language what she already suspected; she would automatically receive a good proportion of the traditional Labour vote, just as she would that of the intelligentsia. It was now a question of attracting the people who would not normally vote for a candidate of the left, and that if it came down to it she would have to deny that she was a socialist at all.

Robinson contacted Harris saying that they were speaking the same language and that they obviously had a lot to talk about. He subsequently arrived at the house and dazzled Mary, Nick and even Bride Rosney with his ebullience, his inherent belief that they could win, and the document he brought with him.

The document restated what he had said in the letter in a far more specific, detailed way. He outlined how they should tackle the media and change people's notions of Mary Robinson as something of a radical. This he claimed would be easy enough. "Your very first press conference must deal with Distortion in a frank and firm fashion as follows: 'Now I want to make something clear. Everybody knows my position on divorce and abortion. But that was Mary Robinson's position. As President I will fully accept the views of the electorate expressed at the referenda. On this I compare my position to that of John F. Kennedy - as President of Ireland I represent the views of the people of Ireland. On every issue. As President my private views don't count."

The Robinsons were impressed but there was one problem to overcome. Harris had long been a controversial figure. His flamboyant go-it-alone style had led to him being called a maverick - albeit a brilliant one - in political circles. They knew that there was no way certain members of the campaign committee would tolerate his presence on the team. And given the fact that he had "resigned" from the Workers' Party less than a month previously in rather acrimonious circumstances, this would also create a problem with the WP who were going to be very valuable allies in certain Dublin constituencies.

They discussed this with Harris and it was decided that it would be best if his place were to remain "discreet" but he continued to provide a wealth of ideas from the sidelines. These ideas were often adopted by Nick and Mary Robinson and by Bride Rosney as their own.

The campaign was officially launched in Limerick on 1 May. Her maiden speech was vigorous and impressive. She said that the office needed to be reformed and even went as far as advocating that the President become the head of the Seanad, which would require specific constitutional adjustment, saying, "if one... receives a mandate from the people I do not think any Government can stand in its way".

She paid polite tribute to the President, Dr. Hillery, describing him as "personable", and openly welcomed the prospect of a Fine Gael candidate saying that it would maximise votes and that "it would benefit me particularly if I could stay ahead of the Fine Gael candidate".

For the next month Mary and Nick Robinson travelled the country reassuring the more conservative rural voters that she would not make the Áras a refuge for gays and lesbians or make Russian a compulsory language, but that she was a caring, compassionate candidate who was trying to break the mould of a rapidly atrophying public position.

She also proved that she was as comfortable condemning the Brussels-based Eurocracy which had neutered rural towns such as Allihies in Co. Cork, as she was at criticising the decision to close down a Women's Aid refuge in Ballymun.

Here it seemed, at last, was a candidate who understood that the people of such built-up working-class areas as Ballymun, Tallaght and Finglas were as isolated and neglected by the people in power as those in the most remote regions of Kerry.

Mary Robinson was profoundly moved and influenced by what

she discovered on her 30,000-mile journey around her own country. Not since her Harvard days had anything like it touched her life so completely. It was a voyage of personal discovery which allowed her to successfully key into people's insecurities about the future, about themselves, and about public figures. In the small towns of Ireland this deeply intellectual woman, who at times in the past seemed so distant from the heart's core of provincial Ireland, established a dynamic which allowed her to see how ordinary Irish people felt about the country.

Fergus Finlay, who was at hand to witness this phenomenon, has observed that it was these ordinary people who were helping Mary Robinson to set her agenda.

"That was the biggest discovery of all," Finlay observes, "that people wanted a President who would be theirs, someone in whom they had invested their faith and their hope. Mary never became anyone's property - by the end of her journey a little bit of Mary Robinson belonged to everyone."

The Robinsons toured until July and the thousands of people they met, each with a differing opinion on the role she was determined to assume, were to provide invaluable experience for when the "real" campaign began later on.

Buoyed by the success of the tour and happy in the knowledge that they had clocked up nearly 20,000 miles before another candidate had even entered the fray, the Robinsons took a short holiday.

The mood improved yet again when Fine Gael announced that Austin Currie was to be their candidate. The frantic Fine Gael search had reached farcical levels when the only two people with any chance of winning the election for them, elder statesmen Garret FitzGerald and Peter Barry had declined all offers to run for office.

Their refusal had left Party leader Alan Dukes and director of elections Jim Mitchell in a desperate quandary. Their frantic search for a candidate began to look like a political version of the Keystone Cops with everybody from Tom O'Donnell, a stalwart of the party right and an embarrassment to the liberal wing, to Kerry playwright John

B. Keane being approached. Even these unlikely choices turned it down. The situation became so desperate that the idea of getting an anonymous man off the street was even mooted at one stage!

With all realistic choices gone and with no well-known Fine Gael person prepared to run in an election they knew they couldn't win, the increasingly beleaguered Alan Dukes was in a perilous situation. Eventually, after much persuading by Mr. Dukes, Austin Currie accepted the challenge on 6 June.

Austin Currie was a stalwart of the Northern Irish political arena and had been a truly respected figure in the SDLP where he proved himself to be a courageous and doughty campaigner. On the Southern front, however, he had only been a TD for a year and was largely unknown even to the Fine Gael party faithful, let alone the rest of the electorate.

If the Robinsons themselves could have chosen the Fine Gael candidate they could not have picked a more suitable figure. He was never going to provide any genuine threat to their campaign and his presence would ensure them the crucial second preference votes that proportional representation guaranteed. Fianna Fáil now had a fight on their hands.

September, however, marked a downward turn in the mood of the Robinson camp. Simmering tension between the Labour and Workers' Party factions was not helped when Workers' Party TD Eamonn Gilmore insisted on being given a place on the campaign committee. This idea was met with anger from Labour who felt that considering that the Workers' Party already had their own committee it was absolutely pointless that Mr. Gilmore should want a place on theirs. Ruairí Quinn steadfastly refused to let him join on the grounds that the Stalinist ethos of Gilmore's party would result in him trying to dictate matters, but eventually on 10 October Quinn relented. Gilmore was officially accepted but in effect had no power as Quinn immediately formed an internal committee of which Gilmore had no knowledge or influence.

Matters were not helped by the growing lack of trust between the

Labour and Robinson camps either. Some members of the Robinson camp were beginning to feel that Labour had no real expectation of winning and were just using Mary Robinson to increase their own profile in areas where they were not traditionally strong. It was felt that they were pushing Mrs. Robinson into these areas merely to garner votes for the next local and general elections. Mary Robinson also felt that too close an association with Labour would alienate her from a significant percentage of the electorate and ghettoise her into the traditional Labour/Workers' Party voting spectrum. She was, after all, an independent candidate.

Labour, on the other hand, felt that they were bending over backwards to accommodate her in her wish to be seen as an independent. They had accepted that the campaign posters and literature were not to be emblazoned with Labour Party logos but they resented what they felt was a calculated freezing out from Robinson. They had, after all, proposed her.

Fergus Finlay, in his account of the election, *Mary Robinson - A President With A Purpose* described the situation: "A view was growing amongst Mary's close advisers that the Labour Party was primarily interested in exploiting Mary's candidacy to broaden their own base of support. They did not see the Party treating the campaign with the same sense of total urgency and total commitment that they themselves felt." He goes on to give the Labour point of view: "Some senior Party members at least were themselves beginning to feel that the Robinsons were beginning to feel that the Party was being 'jollied along' at least until the formal Oireachtas nomination was secured, but to be kept at a distance, simply because the Party was small, and might be offensive to some of the constituency that Mary hoped to attract. Members of the Party involved in the campaign began to notice the efforts that were apparently being made to preserve as much distance as possible between the candidate and the Party."

Central to the friction between the squabbling allies was Bride Rosney who was, after Nick Robinson, the candidate's closest confidante. Ms. Rosney had cut her teeth in trade union politics,

184

traditionally one of the toughest and most acerbic areas of non-legislative lobbying, or as one American trade unionist once put it, "nice guys don't last long in trade unions".

She had known Mary Robinson since 1978 when they met during the Wood Quay Preservation campaign. Dublin's Wood Quay was at the centre of a huge controversy in the late '70s when it was announced that the Government was intent on destroying one of the most valuable Viking settlements in Europe to build a series of office blocks. The protests drew together a wide and various band of vociferous demonstrators. The demonstrators are long gone and in their place stand some of the worst architectural aberrations in the country.

Mary Robinson and Bride Rosney became friends after that, indeed so close did they become that Ms. Rosney was named godmother to one of the Robinson children, Aubrey. Mary Robinson listened to her friend at all times and this position of extreme confidence was undoubtedly resented by some of the Labour team. There was, however, more to the friction than mere jealousy of her proximity to the candidate.

Some of the inner committee felt that Bride Rosney did not believe that Labour was the right vehicle for the candidate's views and that she did not take them seriously enough. They were angered when she told experienced political hands how to do what they felt was their job, such as how to maximise votes in constituencies which she knew nothing about and in which they had spent years campaigning. Given the fact that the members of the committee were experienced and successful in their own fields, tempers were frequently frayed and much valuable time was spent smoothing ruffled feathers.

The problems were further exacerbated when political columnist Geraldine Kennedy revealed that Eoghan Harris was playing a pivotal role in the formulation of the Robinsons' ideas. Dick Spring was horrified at the involvement of Harris but given that he was away on holidays at the time he felt there was little he could do without being seen to be acting dishonourably.

185

Harris returned from holidays in the middle of September to find out that his role in the unfolding drama had been discovered. He then decided that he was no longer "going to stay in the closet".

Not prepared to orchestrate another campaign anonymously, he wrote to the Robinsons:

Dear Mary and Nick,

I slept on the problem. And I'm quite clear on what I have to do. Think of it like this: RTE could offer me a deal today or tomorrow. I would then be free to work in your campaign. But now it seems that I would not be acceptable to the Gang of Four (Spring, Quinn, Rogers and Finlay)...

They should be told to go and f*** themselves. Of course I can see why that's going to be a problem. But I am not going to put myself in a closet.

So count me out if I am in a closet. Naturally I shall do or say nothing that might hurt your campaign. And I am profoundly sorry that I can't go. Bride and Peter (MacMenamin) are great people. And of course, I like you and Nick a lot, and hate to part like this...

The letter had a galvanising effect on the Robinsons and they decided that Harris had become too close an adviser and too good a friend to just drop at the whim of the Party. Nick Robinson, who was perhaps the closest to Harris, met Ruairí Quinn and detailed their position quite simply: Harris stays.

Ruairí Quinn was impressed by the force of Nick Robinson's argument and agreed not to rock the boat. From then on Harris and Quinn met frequently and a potentially divisive stand-off was averted.

Confirmation of the nomination of Brian Lenihan as the Fianna Fáil candidate concentrated everybody's mind but tension stayed in the air.

While Brian Lenihan was still busy reassuring the Party that should he be elected the seat he would leave vacant in Dublin West could be won in the ensuing by-election, Mary Robinson was busy detailing her plans for the office she hoped to inherit from Dr. Hillery.

She was well aware that one of the traditional taboos of Irish society had been emigration and speaking at a rally in Galway she outlined her plans to implement an "emigration task-force". "Almost every family in the country has been affected by emigration," she said. "An elected President's role would be to provide a direct link with emigrants based on informed knowledge of the practical problems faced by them and any agency which supports emigrants."

She called into question the official figure of 46,000 emigrants for 1989 which, she claimed, was "considered by several London based emigration agencies as a serious underestimation". She said that she realised she had an enormous task in convincing Irish voters "that they were the employers of the President". In the same speech she reassured her supporters that she was not worried by the other two candidates, explaining that "the essential focus is on the job and who can do the best job", adding that she was pleased at the way it was shaping up.

Pleased at the way her campaign was shaping up was one thing but she cannot have been pleased at the ever-increasing problems in her own camp.

Following the first media joust between the three candidates on 1 October from which Robinson emerged the victor, the team met to discuss the state of affairs.

A row developed over a statement written by Eoghan Harris which he had released independently. This statement likened Brian Lenihan to "an aging movie queen" and this incensed the Labour team who were trying to ensure that the Robinson campaign was not seen to be resorting to mud-slinging.

This followed a row over Nick Robinson commissioning Lansdowne Marketing to conduct some research on what people thought of Mary's novel approach to the Presidency, and how they would react to a more active Presidency, etc.

Nick Robinson had commissioned the report some months previously, when there were only two candidates in the race but when the bill arrived those who did not know about it were furious. They felt that Nick had no right to be running about commissioning market research behind their backs when campaign funds were scarce enough as it was, but when he explained that the money was going to come out of his own pocket things calmed down somewhat. Some were still irked that they had been kept in the dark about such potentially vital information. There then followed what was rather diplomatically described by Fergus Finlay as "an extremely healthy exchange of opinions which should have happened months earlier".

Nick Robinson and Bride Rosney defended their position, saying that while Nick and Mary had travelled exhaustively around the country from the very onset of the campaign, they felt that the Labour Hierarchy had initially shirked some of their responsibility, and that it was only now, when she was picking up steam, that they were prepared to give her the help and support which she had needed from the beginning.

By this they meant that the fund-raising had not been particularly enthusiastic and that the grassroots never seemed to be properly informed of her whereabouts.

According to Finlay, those present were genuinely "shocked", given that they "had for months harboured the conviction that the Robinsons wanted to keep their distance from the Party, in the belief that association would damage their chances".

This cathartic exchange of views worked wonders for everybody and after both sides had established themselves in a context that the other could understand, effective working relationships were restored.

This was just as well given that a few days later on 4 October *The Irish Times* ran a piece with the headline "Robinson Would Promote Gay Rights". The opening paragraph read, "Mrs. Mary Robinson has said that she would actively promote the use of contraceptives and defend the rights of minority groups such as the gay community, if elected on November 7th".

These remarks were lifted from an edition of *Hot Press* magazine which that morning ran an interview with Mary Robinson that threatened to blow her hard-earned "safe" image out of the water.

Although primarily a music magazine, *Hot Press* has always aspired to being more than just another rock publication. It worked at developing a political hard edge, recruiting figures such as Eamon McCann and Michael D. Higgins to write regular columns.

It was for this very reason that it seemed like a good idea for Mary Robinson to do an interview with them. The readership was, after all, predominantly 18 to 25-year-olds, and she was aware that this was a vital demographic niche to tap into.

Mary Robinson's potential nemesis came in the form of the quietly spoken Liam Fay, a staff writer with the magazine.

As far as Fay was concerned the interview was a successful one. He had spent an hour in her house and the conversation was wide-ranging and forthright.

Known as she was for her outspoken views on so many aspects of Irish life, they spoke about the role of the Catholic Church, the judiciary and other staples of Irish society.

The statement that caused all the furore came, however, while talking about a topic which returned like some old familiar tune to haunt the weary candidate: condoms.

Liam Fay asked: "To a large extent, the personality of a Presidency is defined by the public functions and occasions which the President chooses to attend. Would you, for example, perform the official opening of the condom stall at the Virgin Megastore Store?"

At the time it was illegal to sell condoms outside certain pharmacies or permanent IFPA (Irish Family Planning Association) clinics.

Mary Robinson's reply was: "Yes. This is a very young country and I think it would be very helpful to have a President that was aware of what young people would be thinking."

This answer was consistent with the tone of the rest of the interview. In her book on the election campaign, *Candidate*, the interview was described by Emily O'Reilly as "an apparently thoughtless romp through a myriad of issues, felling holy cows as she went, the Church, the judiciary, family planning inadequacies, homosexuality nothing was sacred".

Having written up the interview and put the issue to bed, Fay thought no more on the matter until the morning the issue was released. The first signs of the gathering storm were remarks made by Gay Byrne on his early morning radio show.

As Liam Fay explained: "I had heard Byrne on the radio that morning and he was saying how Brian Lenihan would never say such things, but I didn't really pay much attention to him, to be honest... It was only when I got into the office later on that morning that I discovered Brenda O'Hanlon (a member of the Robinson team) had been on the phone looking for a transcript and copy of the tape, which was very unusual.

"We discovered why when we listened to *News At One* on Radio 1 that afternoon and heard [Mary Robinson] saying that she had a copy of the interview and that she had been misquoted. Niall Stokes (the editor of *Hot Press*) asked me to go home and find the tape and play it for him. I had just moved flat at the time and I initially could not find the tape anywhere! I eventually found it under my bed and after playing it to Niall he agreed that I had quoted her verbatim."

Mary Robinson made precious few errors of judgement throughout the campaign but her decision to go on the radio show to defend herself threatened to be the most grievous. It was also exactly what some members of the committee were afraid of. They were confident that given the limited circulation of *Hot Press* the whole débâcle would eventually run out of steam, if Mary Robinson would just let it lie.

Their fears turned to alarm when they heard Mrs. Robinson on the radio giving her worst media performance of the campaign.

When asked by presenter Shane Kenny if she would, indeed, be prepared to open such a condom stall in the Virgin Megastore she replied rather bafflingly, "Yes, I have the text of the interview in front of me. I did not say Yes at the start of the question. I was asked in a kind of trendy way about the Virgin Megastore and I said... this is a very young country and I think that it would be helpful if the President was in touch with what young people were doing... I would not, as President, be associated with something that is not legal."

Mary Robinson clearly floundered for the rest of the interview and was at pains to point out that she would "use the Áras to promote family life", that she was a church-going Catholic who attended mass with her family and that she had been happily married for the last 20 years. She then claimed that if she had actually said Yes, it was merely to prove that she understood the first part of the question. It was, she said, "a mannerism Yes", not an affirmative answer.

The journalists at *Hot Press*, listening to the interview were furious. Liam Fay recalls: "The clear implication was that we had given her a copy of the tape when in actual fact the 'text' of the interview which she referred to was merely a copy of *Hot Press*."

Niall Stokes immediately contacted Robinson and told her to stop claiming that she had been misquoted when it was clear on the tape that she actually had said Yes, and in comments after the initial controversy Mary Robinson merely claimed that she had been misinterpreted.

An opinion poll released on 1 October had shown Austin Currie to be trailing in third place with an abysmal 17 per cent. Jim Mitchell and his colleagues were aware that the only way for Currie to claw himself back up in the opinion polls was if one of the candidates made some dreadful error. This, they hoped, was what they had been praying for.

Fine Gael Press Officer, Peter White, immediately contacted *Six One News* and secured a slot for Currie to appear that night and comment on the Robinson/*Hot Press* interview. They wanted him to go and, according to one of the campaigners, "sock it to Mary Robinson". It was their only hope.

Austin Currie had been campaigning in Swords that day and a statement had been prepared back in Fine Gael's Mount Street offices for him. The statement was a clever one. Rather than have Currie go on air and berate her for the insensitivity of her remarks they planned on having Currie ask what all the fuss was about? After all, these were the views for which she was well known and by voting for her the electorate would be endorsing these views.

It was one of the few chances that Currie would have of taking a genuine chunk out of Robinson's lead and their campaign team knew that now was not the time for him to get cold feet.

It was not a view shared by Currie himself. It is important to understand that Currie is a graduate of the Northern Irish school of political manoeuvring, where a badly turned phrase could cost a politician a great deal more than his seat. This had instilled in him a very understandable reluctance to fire from the hip when it came to making statements.

The statement was read over the phone to him in Swords but he refused to officially endorse anything until he had read it himself. He was aware that a sizeable proportion of the Fine Gael liberal wing harboured a secret (and on occasions not so secret) empathy with Mary Robinson. He was also aware that he was having a tough enough time convincing undecideds that they should vote for him without losing any of the vote he could supposedly take for granted.

He also felt that at some stage down the line he would probably enter into a vote transfer deal with her and he did not want to risk that deal by unduly annoying Robinson and her handlers. Currie still felt that he could finish second and he was loathe to do anything that might jeopardise that.

After seeing a faxed copy of the statement and deciding that he was definitely not going to put his name to it he set about drafting a new statement of his own.

This statement, considerably safer and more cautious than the original one, called into question Mary Robinson's assertion that she would be able to look any Taoiseach in the eye and "tell him to back off".

Although Robinson was on questionable constitutional ground she had made this assertion before and what Currie needed was a response that would capture the electorate's imagination, not an esoteric debate on constitutional law.

It was too late by this stage for Currie to get out to the RTE studios in Donnybrook from Swords, so Fine Gael brought in Garret FitzGerald to attack the other two candidates on the Northern question. FitzGerald did a competent job but the public had heard it all before.

Yet again, Austin Currie's reluctance to get down and trade political blows had further weakened his chances of success in the election.

Currie eventually released his statement on 8 October. It was bland and ineffectual and was greeted with widespread apathy. He claimed that in making the remarks she did she was playing into the hands of Fianna Fáil and that she "should not allow herself be pushed by the extreme fringes of the left wing beyond sound legal judgement".

The mild tone of the statement, coupled with his remark that, "we can all make mistakes and Mrs. Robinson can be forgiven for making her mistake" was generally derided as the words of someone afraid to take the rose by the thorns.

The release of the statement was also overshadowed by the release of an opinion poll the same day which showed Robinson at 32 per cent while Currie was behind on 19 per cent.

This was the first opinion poll to be released since the *Hot Press* interview was published and it seemed to show that the semi-scandal of the interview had done her no harm at all.

In fact, the poll had been conducted in the days before the interview was released but it still gave the impression of a candidate whose momentum was now becoming that of a runaway train.

The real Fine Gael attack on Mary Robinson's credibility ultimately had to come from the Director of Elections, Jim Mitchell, when he called her "the acceptable face of socialism" in Ireland and tried to exploit the Workers' Party endorsement of her to initiate a red scare - reminiscent of those red scares of the late 1960s - amongst the voters.

This backfired on both Mitchell and his charge when Proinsias De Rossa denounced the claims as an "ugly and sinister development in the campaign... we (the Workers' Party) support her because she represents a new and progressive strand in Irish politics" and he further pilloried Mitchell as a representative of "the discredited past".

The Robinson team stayed sensibly aloof during the skirmish, their only comment on Mitchell's foolhardy swipe was to dismiss it as "not very credible. Probably said in the heat of the moment". Even Fianna Fáil said little on the situation. Although past masters at ensuring that any mistake by an opponent was brought to public attention as an example of their scurrilous character, they knew that Brian Lenihan was well ahead in the opinion polls and they did not want to embroil their man in any potentially messy cat-fight.

Mary Robinson herself was also a paragon of diplomacy when asked at a press conference whether the apparent ill-health of Brian Lenihan would affect his execution of his duties were he to be elected, saying that while it would probably be an issue in other countries, "I think that we might be more kindly and humane. It is not, from my point of view, an appropriate issue on which to comment."

What nobody was to know at the time she made that remark was that within less than a week, the whole Fianna Fáil campaign team would have considerable cause for worry.

In May 1990, Jim Duffy, a student of politics at University College Dublin wrote a letter to Brian Lenihan requesting an interview as part of his MA thesis on Political Science. The letter detailed the areas which Duffy wanted to talk to him about, namely:

1) The nature of the relationship between the Taoiseach and the President

2) The different approach to the office by successive Presidents

3) The Presidency as viewed from Leinster House during his period in the Oireachtas

4) Specific incidents involving the Presidency (e.g. the allegation that President de Valera convinced Kevin Boland not to resign in 1969; de Valera's support for Jack Lynch during the arms crisis, etc.).

Given Lenihan's long-standing and genuinely admirable tradition of assisting students and academics alike in their studies, Duffy was not surprised when contacted by Brian Spain, Lenihan's private secretary, and informed that Lenihan would meet him on the afternoon of 17 May.

On arrival at Leinster House, Duffy was struck by how unwell the Tánaiste looked. After repeated reassurances that he was fine the interview commenced. It ranged from specific incidents such as the resignation of Cearbhall Ó Dálaigh to his general observations on the position of the Presidency itself.

The interview seemed to be following the normal pattern of such academic exercises: heavily detailed, immensely helpful to the person doing the research and of no interest to the general public whatsoever.

But that all changed when the topic of conversation turned to discussing the allegations that senior members of Fianna Fáil, Brian Lenihan among them, tried to persuade President Hillery not to dissolve the Dáil during the budget crisis of 1982.

That year saw the Garret FitzGerald-led Coalition collapse after losing a vote on the new budgetary changes they planned to make that February. Charles Haughey's position as the new leader of Fianna Fáil was already under a certain amount of threat and it would have been enormously beneficial to him if Dr. Hillery refused to dissolve the Dáil and asked Mr. Haughey to form a new, emergency government instead, thus saving the country the trouble and expense of another general election.

There had never been any real doubt that certain people had tried to get through to President Hillery but it was never known if any of them had actually succeeded. So it was with astonished ears that Duffy heard Brian Lenihan say, "Oh yeah, I got through to him, all right, and he told us to lay off." Duffy then filed it away as an interesting nugget for when he was preparing his thesis, and not as the remarks that were going to cause one of the most bizarre and dramatic changes in political fortunes in recent Irish history.

He gave the issue no more thought until 16 October when at a question and answer session in UCD, Brian Lenihan was asked by Seamus Kennedy, the then chairman of the college's Fine Gael branch, if he had ever made any telephone calls to President Hillery on that fateful evening in January 1982. Lenihan denied that he ever had and the issue would have been forgotten only for the fact that Jim Duffy was in attendance and he knew that this was not the answer he had been given in May.

Duffy told some friends of his about the difference between the two answers given by Brian Lenihan on the two separate occasions. Brian Lenihan was quizzed again when he appeared on RTE's *Questions And Answers* show some days later.

The morning the programme was due to be recorded the *Irish Press* published an interview with Brian Lenihan as part of their series on the Presidential candidates and Lenihan again denied that he had made any phone calls saying, "I didn't do it, not personally. He [President Hillery] didn't discuss it with me anyway. The President was very independent at the time and he did not discuss it with me."

Jim Duffy was positive at the time that he did not want to make public the relevant portions of the tape of the interview as he realised that this would be a dreadful breach of confidentiality, but he was furious at what he saw as Lenihan's blatant untruths which were going to discredit the relevant parts of his thesis when it was eventually published.

By this stage Duffy had told several of his friends in Fine Gael about it and it was arranged to have a plant in the audience of the *Questions And Answers* show who would, again, ask Lenihan whether he had taken any part in the attempted influencing of a President.

During the course of the panel debate Garret FitzGerald, who had been with Dr. Hillery in the Áras at the time of the mysterious phone calls, spoke of "a series of phone calls" made to the President without actually naming anybody in particular. A typical session of political jousting then ensued between the two old adversaries, Lenihan and FitzGerald with Lenihan saying, "that is fictional Garret". This continued until Brian Murphy, a friend of Duffy's and a member of the Austin Currie campaign team, interrupted and asked Lenihan, "Did you, or did you not, make a phone call, or phone calls, to Áras an Uachtaráin in that period", to which Lenihan replied unequivocally, "No. I didn't at all, that never happened. I want to assure you that it never happened."

Lenihan's campaign team, especially Bertie Aherne, were mildly puzzled by this seemingly unusual interest in a relatively forgotten paragraph of Irish politics, but there was no major concern, or any knowledge that the dam was about to burst on them.

Jim Duffy was still doubtful about whether he had the moral right to publish such confidential material, but by now his rather public wracking of his conscience had come to the attention of several young Fianna Fáilers who, after telling Aherne of the possible existence of such an offending tape were instructed to go and find Duffy and his tape. Duffy had approached several senior academics in the college for guidance and a possible solution to his dilemma, and while none of them actually advocated his release of the tape, only one, RTE presenter Brian Farrell, warned him against it.

Duffy had aspirations to being a political journalist and had already written a series on the Presidency for *The Irish Times*, who were aware of the existence of the tape. The day after the *Questions And Answers* show he rang Denis Coughlan, a senior political reporter with the newspaper and told him that he felt he could not publish the portions of the tape.

This assertion failed to ease his mind, however. He was under pressure from some Fine Gael friends of his to release the tape and he knew that he was sitting on something that could conceivably change the face of the election.

On Tuesday evening he finally played the tape for Denis Coughlan and the editor of *The Irish Times*, Conor Brady.

Positive that the voice on the tape was indeed that of the Tánaiste, Brady persuaded Duffy to let them run a small story on page one, saying that they now had positive proof that Lenihan had admitted to making the phone calls but they would not reveal the source or where he had got his information from.

The publication of this story convinced Fianna Fáil that it was indeed Duffy and they made frantic efforts to get to him before any of the other political parties and persuade him not to release the tape. They could give him very good reasons for not releasing it. Firstly, they could persuade him that by releasing the tape he would be changing irrevocably the way in which such academic interviews were conducted. Never again would a politician agree to help out a student if the politician felt that the student would run off to the newspapers at the first sign of a decent quote. Secondly, they could appeal to his own sense of self-preservation; it was well known that Duffy wanted to forge a career for himself as a journalist. How could potential sources expect to trust him when he could so obviously not keep a confidence?

The question now was whether they could get to him before anyone else did. In addition to scouring the grounds of UCD and all his known haunts they leaked his name to RTE.

Duffy knew that there were agents of Fianna Fáil looking for him but what really infuriated him was when he heard his name on the radio. Duffy took refuge in the chaplaincy of UCD and contacted Conor Brady and told him that he was now prepared to release the tapes. The pressure Fianna Fáil had put on the young student, and their eagerness to keep the tapes away from the public eye, had blown back in their faces.

Secure in the knowledge that he was not going to suffer any academic repercussions, he then went to Hayes & Sons, solicitors who acted for *The Irish Times*. There he met Conor Brady, and after confirming that he would not be open to any legal problems he discussed the most effective way to release the tape.

A hasty press conference was arranged for Thursday 25 October in the Westbury Hotel.

The assembled journalists were each given a transcript of the tape which read:

DUFFY: I believe there were eight (8) phone calls made.
LENIHAN: Well, there weren't eight, I think there were two or three. There were two or three certainly.
DUFFY: But you made a phone call?
LENIHAN: Oh, I did.
DUFFY: Sylvester Barrett made one.

LENIHAN: That's right.

DUFFY: Did any of the phone calls get through to the President straight?

LENIHAN: Oh yeah, I mean, I got through to him, I remember talking to him and he wanted to... There was no doubt about it in his mind, in fact, looking back on it, it was a mistake on our part because Paddy Hillery would be very - what's the word - strict or conventional in that way you know, he wouldn't want to start breaking new gr... he's not that sort of man. The sort of fellow that wouldn't, it didn't, break new ground. But of course Charlie was gung ho. And there is an argument, you know, under that. We'll have to improve the phraseology of that.

DUFFY: Definitely, definitely... I understand from a civil servant that Mr. Haughey went to the Áras himself. Is that the case?

LENIHAN: I only know about the phone call. I remember distinctly and I have described to you the phone call. I don't know whether Haughey went up himself personally after that.

Fianna Fáil's worst nightmares had come true. Here was their Tánaiste and Presidential candidate not only making a liar out of himself but he was also implicating his boss, Charlie Haughey as well.

That evening, Director of Elections, Bertie Aherne, and the Government Press Officer, P.J. Mara, listened in growing horror as the tape was broadcast on RTE News. It seemed to them that the candidate had only one viable option: to resign.

Lenihan himself had no intention of doing any such thing and when Seán Duignan from RTE News approached Niamh O'Connor of the Fianna Fáil Press Office about Lenihan going on the Six-One News that night Lenihan immediately agreed.

Mara found time to briefly advise Lenihan on how he should deal with the interview. Look directly into the camera, he said, and address the Irish people.

If Mary Robinson going on the news exactly three weeks earlier was risky, Brian Lenihan doing so was potentially political suicide. An

RTE floor-manager remembers Brian Lenihan asking which camera he would be on, and getting increasingly agitated when told not to worry about such technical matters, all would be well. Brian Lenihan did find the right camera and indeed spent much of his time looking directly into it. Every sitting room in Ireland stared into the eyes of a man whose political career was now in serious trouble. The public knew it, his handlers knew it. In fact it seemed as if the only person in the country who was not aware of it was Brian Lenihan himself.

It was disastrous. Lenihan's claim that on "mature recollection" he was now certain that he did not, in fact, make any phone calls to the President, failed to convince most people. His repeated use of this phrase "mature recollection" was embarrassing and it entered the national political lexicon. He certainly wasn't heard using the other catch phrase for which he was so well known. That phrase was "no problem!"

There were mixed emotions in the Robinson camp. The first reaction from some of the team was that they should go in for the kill immediately. They felt that the nation was still too shocked to start feeling any sympathy for the candidate and now was the time to finish him off.

Mary Robinson, however, disagreed with this thinking because according to Fergus Finlay, "She quite simply felt a lot of human sympathy for the dilemma in which Lenihan had placed himself and that is what she expressed."

The only thing that they could do was leave it alone and hope that Lenihan would find himself increasingly alienated from the electorate and his own Party. It was for this reason that Dick Spring did not want to table a no-confidence motion, fearing that the Party faithful would only rally around and support the marginalised Tánaiste.

There was immense pressure on the candidate to resign both from the campaign and from the Party.

Mary Robinson spent the weekend campaigning along the south west of the country. She was gratified to see 2,000 people wait in the rain to hear her speak and although she made the mistake of posing for photographers in Listowel with a toy phone in her hand, thus appearing to make a cruel jibe at Lenihan's situation, the photographs never appeared in any of the national newspapers so any potential for her to be seen gloating over her rival's misfortune was averted.

The day after the mass rally the Robinson campaign received some more good news. An *Irish Press*/IMS poll showed that only 18 per cent of the electorate believed Brian Lenihan's "mature recollection", while 51 per cent now claimed that they were going to be voting for Robinson.

On the face of it this seemed incredibly good news and many members of the team were delighted that it basically reversed all previous polls. But Robinson was aware of the saying "a week is a long time in politics" and cautioned her staff that, "if he can fall so quickly he can come back up again just as quickly".

Everybody would have been happier if the election was to be held the next week, but with the ten-day wait they knew that if Fianna Fáil were to do anything to Lenihan it could spark a huge sympathy vote. Which is exactly what Fianna Fáil did.

At the first opportunity Fine Gael made it known that they were going to table a motion of no confidence in the Government.

The coalition between Fianna Fáil and The Progressive Democrats was an uneasy one and Charles Haughey knew that if they could bail out and increase their profile they would jump at the chance.

Fine Gael's reason for the no confidence motion was "Lenihan's deliberate misleading of the public, the fact that Ministers Bertie Ahern, Ray Burke and Padraig Flynn had publicly backed what he said, and the fact that the Taoiseach had branded Garret FitzGerald a liar in relation to the Duffy tapes". The PDs had been set up in reaction to the tradition of Fianna Fáil shenanigans; they liked to think of themselves as the antithesis of the old back-slapping, hail-fellow-well-met style of parties, and in the event of such a motion they would have no choice but to vote against their Government partners.

The only possible way to avoid such a debate would be if Brian Lenihan were to resign. Brian Lenihan was counselled by his family and close friends to make no such move.

He was campaigning in an area where he was particularly strong, and the sight of so many faithful supporters was convincing him that he would indeed be able to weather the storm.

Charles Haughey was under pressure from all sides. He knew that the Party was unlikely to come well out of a general election and he knew that although the only way of avoiding one was if Brian Lenihan stepped down, it was abundantly clear that he would not.

On the Bank Holiday Monday before the presidential election, the Fianna Fáil leader called a crisis meeting of his cabinet ministers. Brian Lenihan was not present. Lenihan and Haughey met the next morning and Haughey told his old friend and political confidant that the Progressive Democrats were putting him under severe pressure and, while the Party would stand by whatever decision he made, maybe he should consider resigning. For the good of the Party.

Lenihan appreciated his boss's position and promised to think it over. But it was while in the Dáil that his mind was made up for him. His Fianna Fáil colleague, Vincent Brady, told him that the situation was extremely serious and that he would have to resign. He then offered the beleaguered man a prepared letter of resignation. Lenihan objected to being treated like this by a junior colleague and went back out onto the campaign trail. He then heard on RTE News that the Minister of State, Michael Smith, had issued a statement congratulating him on his decision to protect the Party's position and step down. In much the same way that they had forced Jim Duffy into a position where he was angered into releasing the tapes which sparked all the trouble, Fianna Fáil pushed Lenihan into a corner where he decided that if he were to go down, he would go down fighting.

On the way back to Dublin he rang his Director of Elections, Bertie Ahern, and told him that he was not resigning. The lines were drawn, something would have to give. Inevitably, it was Brian Lenihan.

The next day, after giving Lenihan another chance to resign, which was again refused, Haughey told the Dáil: "I regret to inform the House that this evening I requested the Tánaiste and Minister for Defence,

202

Mr. Brian Lenihan, TD, to resign as a member of the Government and that he failed to comply with my request. Accordingly, I propose to exercise my constitutional prerogative and advise the President to terminate his appointment as a member of the Government."

It was exactly what the Robinson camp was dreading. The rank and file of Fianna Fáil had been surprisingly sluggish in their campaigning for Lenihan, already secure in their belief that he was going to walk the election.

Now that he was in a position of such grave trouble they would waste no time in trying to ensure the election of the most popular politician of his generation.

Mary Robinson had maintained a dignified stance throughout the tapes scandal, saying "the phone call should not be blown out of all proportion or detract from the decency of Brian Lenihan's record of public service or be allowed to plunge the Government into a crisis".

Given the attempt by Fine Gael to smear her and the obvious difficulties surrounding Lenihan it seemed that Robinson was the only candidate behaving in a manner befitting someone hoping to be the First Citizen. Would Brian Lenihan now sail into the Áras on a great tide of sympathy and irrational affection?

Mary Robinson also had the added burden of three high profile TV engagements in the last week of the campaign. She had been due to go on *Today Tonight* the day the Lenihan tape affair broke, but she consented to postpone her appearance so that the current affairs show could discuss that matter.

This would have been ideal if she had been still in second place, but now that she was the favourite she had to try to consolidate her position rather than merely hope to try and catch up. She was also exhausted. She had started her campaign in May and the toll was beginning to show. She now had two *Today Tonight* specials (the planned debate between the three candidates and her re-scheduled personal appearance, and the *Late Late Show*, which planned a special with the candidates and their spouses.

Just as she was preparing herself on the tour bus for the first *Today*

Tonight appearance she got word of remarks made about her at a Fianna Fáil campaign meeting the previous night. The meeting had taken place in the presence of Brian Lenihan in the Talbot Hotel in Wexford town and a report in the *Wexford People* quoted the Wexford Fianna Fáil TD, John Browne's denunciation of her as the "biggest hypocrite of the campaign... She's pro-divorce, pro-contraception and pro-abortion. Is she going to open an abortion referral clinic in Áras an Uachtaráin? That's what I'd like to know".

The reaction to her performance in the interview is widely divergent. Fergus Finlay says, "Her anger, controlled and yet tangible, came across in the interview, and enabled her to deal clearly with the whole issue of abortion and the right to information forcefully and with absolute clarity. When it was broadcast, members of the committee who had watched it believed it to have been the best interview given by any candidate for office in many years."

Under the last minute advice of Eoghan Harris she launched her most scathing attack of the campaign on Lenihan and she was visibly drained afterwards as all the tension and fatigue of the previous six months caught up with her.

It seemed to Mary Robinson that all the problems she had avoided so far were sneaking up on her now. A few days earlier Fine Gael TD for Carlow-Kilkenny, Phil Hogan, sent a letter out to his constituents repeating the red scare tactic saying, "A vote for Mary Robinson will be interpreted as a vote for Workers' Party policies which are not in the best interest of the country." Family Solidarity, the right wing "family values" group, sent a letter to thousands of voters urging them to vote for Lenihan and/or Currie. Meanwhile, Brian Lenihan was creeping back up in the opinion polls. The day after her *Today Tonight* performance an *Irish Times* poll showed that she was down to 43 per cent of the vote with Lenihan four percentage points behind on 39 per cent.

The *Late Late Show* appearance, set for the same night on which these worrying new figures were released was a cause of some concern for the Robinsons. Ann Lenihan, having stood beside her husband for so many years, was well versed in how to deal with the media while it didn't really matter at this stage how Anita Currie did. But Nick was a different matter. He had been interviewed by the media on many occasions, not just as the husband of Mary Robinson, but in his own right as an authority on Irish architecture and as a collector. However, he had very little experience of such high-profile television exposure, and a visibly uncomfortable Nick would not bode well for Mary. There was the worry that, through no fault of his own, he could come across as being a stuffy "West Brit" who might get overly excited about swan-neck pediments or some other architectural delight, and that the general public might not be able to relate to him.

As it turned out, Eoghan Harris had coached him well. He could have had no better coach. He charmed the audience with a story about the piper Seamus Ennis, whom Nick had met through Ann Lane. They couldn't have picked a better person to use in a story. What could be more Irish than the late Seamus Ennis? The very fact that Nick knew such a well-known traditional music figure surprised many people and any fear that Nick Robinson was "different" was put to rest.

Unfortunately, Mary herself was not quite so convincing and Gay Byrne told the audience how she had chastised him during the break for making the conversation "too political". He then put it to her that "Fianna Fáil put out a statement to say that in October 1990 you said: 'I am a socialist - the task is to build the socialist movement. We want banks nationalised and building land controlled'."

Robinson laughed and denied the claim, but the next day a report appeared in *The Irish Times* which read in part, "the quote by Mr. Byrne did not accurately reflect the statement issued early yesterday by the Minister for Social Welfare, who said that according to an article published last October she had made 'such a statement when she first stood for election to the Dáil' and that was in 1982."

The material used by Dr. Woods appeared in the *Phoenix* magazine of 5 October, but would seem to be based on an interview given by Mrs. Robinson to *The Irish Times* in March 1982. In this she spoke of her need for a social and political framework for her commitment and her discontent in approaching political problems as a liberal. She welcomed the Labour Party's decision not to participate in coalition at that time and said: "The task now is to use the existing pressures to build the socialist movement. The factors operating now are those which can lead to a serious political alternative. It's the crunch point for Labour..."

Mrs. Robinson went on in the interview: "We need to be much tougher about our own policies. We want employment; we have to cost it. We want banks nationalised, taxation reformed, building land controlled..."

This might very well have been another untimely blow were it not for the unwitting, but very welcome intervention of Environment Minister, Padraig Flynn.

Padraig Flynn in RTE's Castlebar studio was on a panel with Labour TD Brendan Howlin, and the chairman of the Progressive Democrats, Michael McDowell, on RTE's *Saturday View*, presented by Rodney Rice. Ronan O'Donoghue who was producing the show was hoping that this volatile mix would make for some interesting radio listening amid the plethora of facts, figures and statistics that perpetually clog up pre-election radio. The show got more than it bargained for.

Flynn had been instructed to go on the offensive against Robinson but seemed to take his brief rather too literally when, mid-way through the programme he launched an astonishingly vitriolic attack on Robinson saying: "She was pretty well constructed in this campaign by her handlers, the Labour Party and the Workers' Party. Of course it doesn't always suit if you get labelled a socialist, because that's a very narrow focus in this country - so she has to try and have it both ways. She has to have new clothes and her new look and her new hairdo and she has the new interest in family, being a mother and all that kind of thing. But none of us you know, none of us who knew Mary Robinson very well in previous incarnations ever heard her claiming to be a great wife and mother."

Rodney Rice looked around the studio in astonishment at the other

206

guests as Flynn's disembodied voice trilled around the room. McDowell tried to interrupt but Flynn was in full force. He continued, "Mary Robinson reconstructs herself to fit the fashion of the time, so we have this thing about you can be substituted at will, whether it's the pro-socialist thing, or pro-contraception, or pro-abortion - whatever it is.

"But at least we should know. Mary Robinson is a socialist, she says, and has admitted it previously. Now she may have changed her mind, and if she has changed her mind, so be it. But at least she should tell us that she has changed her mind, and not be misleading us."

McDowell listened intently throughout this tirade, and then, in one of the most riveting pieces of recent Irish radio slammed into Minister Flynn and told him that he should have some manners for once. He called the attack "disgusting" and demanded an immediate apology.

Realising the gravity of the accusations he had made, a statement was released by Flynn later that evening which said: "I am happy to state that Mrs. Mary Robinson's family life is exemplary. It was never my intention to suggest otherwise. I deeply regret that anything I may have said during the lively exchange may have inadvertently conveyed the contrary view."

But it was too little too late. Mary Robinson, knowing that these were the actions of a desperate man, was able to publicly laugh it off, although privately it must have caused her great anger and irritation. Nothing has meant more to Mary Robinson than her family. Legal career, Senate career, Dáil elections, European committees and presidential election, all took a firm second place to her commitment to her family.

But in a curious way Padraig Flynn was to play a most significant role in the election of Mary Robinson - a scenario that none but the most politically naïve might ever have imagined possible. The public revulsion caused by his remarks nullified the effect of the forecast sympathy vote for Brian Lenihan, and it was the final nail in the coffin for a Party determined to hold on to the highest office in the land.

The only remaining hitch came on the second day of polling in the RDS when 41,732 votes went missing. This cut Mary Robinson's lead over Brian Lenihan down by three thousand, but any fears of an unprecedented loss of the votes were stopped when it was discovered that these were the total number of votes counted in the Wicklow constituency.

The first count showed Mary Robinson to be 82,219 votes behind Brian Lenihan, but with Currie's transfers still to be distributed this was a very healthy situation for Mary Robinson. The final opinion poll of the campaign placed her at level pegging with Brian Lenihan, each with 43 per cent, and Currie at 14 per cent.

The final count on 9 November showed that Mary Robinson had won by a margin of 86,557 - a genuinely impressive result. She had won every constituency in Dublin and took, in total, 25 of the 41 constituencies nationwide. She also took both constituencies in her native Mayo. Across the country Fine Gael votes transferred to Mary Robinson by a margin of over five to one. Fergus Finlay points out that her margin of victory was eight times bigger than that secured by Eamon de Valera in the presidential election of 1966.

As a key member of the team which helped secure that victory Fergus Finlay summed it up as follows:

"The presidential election of 1990 was a triumph in many ways. It was a triumph of dedication and commitment over the huge resources and bigger machines of the largest political parties in the State. It was a triumph of imagination and energy over the stale ideas of stuck-in-the-mud, complacent organisations. It was a triumph of style and substance."

The result had a major impact on Irish political life. The system, as Mrs. Robinson pointed out in her victory speech, has been rocked, not just as she suggested by the hand that rocked the cradle, but by a great many hands who had never even seen a cradle.

Within days of her victory Alan Dukes had been replaced as leader of Fine Gael. Questions were being asked, yet again, within Fianna

Fáil about Charles Haughey's leadership. The party began a major policy evaluation, with a view to more open pluralist values - the sort of values Mary Robinson had been preaching since her election to the Senate in 1969. Even the Labour Party was not immune to soul-searching in the policy area. A rightward shift towards social democracy would soon see the party back in Government with its leader, Dick Spring, as Tánaiste and Minister for Foreign Affairs.

The Minister for Tourism and Transport, Seamus Brennan, had said during the campaign that a victory for Mary Robinson "would be claimed by Labour and the Workers' Party as a great victory for the Left". No such claim was made. There was no precedent for the effect the presidential election of 1990 had on Irish politics. An *Irish Times* editorial of 10 November struck the right note:

"Reputations have been put on the line. Party philosophies have been put up for judgement. Party leaderships have been enhanced in some cases; threatened in others."

Fine Gael offered the view during the campaign that the election result would make a statement about Ireland and the Irish to the rest of the world. Mary Robinson preferred the view that it would make a statement to the Irish about themselves.

"The Ireland I will be representing is a new Ireland," she said in her inauguration address, "open, tolerant, inclusive. Many of you who voted for me did so without sharing all my views. This, I believe, is a significant signal of change, a sign, however modest, that we have already passed the threshold to a new, pluralist Ireland."

Though Mary Robinson played no small part in pushing Ireland headlong over that threshold, her role at the forefront of Ireland's pluralist crusade went mostly unrecognised. How quickly that changed after she stood in Dublin Castle amid the trappings of State to take the Presidential oath and witness her destiny draw near.

BIBLIOGRAPHY

BOOKS, ARTICLES AND PAMPHLETS

Browne, Terence, *Ireland A Social and Cultural History*, (London: Fontana, 1985).

Browne, Vincent (ed.), *The Magill Book of Irish Politics*, (Dublin: Magill Publications, 1981).

Brynn, Edward, Crown and Castle: *British Rule in Ireland 1800-1830*, (Dublin: The O'Brien Press, 1978).

Burtchaell, G.D. and Sadlier, T.U. (eds.), *Alumni Dublinenses, a Register of Students, Graduates... of Trinity College in the University of Dublin, 1594 to 1846. 2nd edition with supplement 1846 to 1860*, (Dublin, 1935).

Chubb, Basil, *The Government and Politics of Ireland*, (Stanford: Stanford University Press, 1970).

Chubb, Basil, *The Constitution and Constitutional Change in Ireland*, (Dublin: Institute of Public Administration, 1978).

Cooney, John, *The Crozier and the Dail: Church and State in Ireland 1922-1986*, (Cork : Mercier Press, 1986).

Corish, Brendan, *The New Republic*, (Dublin: Irish Labour Party, 1968).

Collins, Stephen, *Spring and the Labour Story*, (Dublin: O'Brien Press, 1993).

Dublin University Calendar 1965-6 and 1968-9, (Dublin: Hodges Figgis, 1966 and 1969).

Farrell, Brian, *Dáil Deputies: "The 1969 Generation"*, Economic and Social Review: 3 (1970-71), pp. 309-27.

Fennell, Desmond, *The State of the Nation: Ireland Since the Sixties*, (Dublin: Ward River Press, 1983).

Fennell, Desmond, (ed.) *The Changing Face of Catholic Ireland*, (London: Geoffrey Chapman, 1968).

Finlay, Fergus, *Mary Robinson, A President with a Purpose*, (Dublin: O'Brien Press, 1990).

FitzGerald, Garret, *Towards a New Ireland*, (Dublin: Gill & Macmillan 1972).

FitzGerald, Garret, *All in a Life, An Autobiography*, (Dublin: Gill & Macmillan, 1991).

211

Gallagher, Michael, *The Presidency of the Republic of Ireland: Implications of the "Donegan Affair"*, Parliamentary Affairs 30:4, pp. 373-84.

Gallagher, Michael, *The Irish Labour Party In Transition 1957-82*, (Manchester: Manchester University Press, 1982).

Garvin, Thomas, *The Irish Senate*, (Dublin: Institute of Public Administration, 1969).

Gillett, Eric, (ed.), *Elizabeth Ham by Herself*, (London: Faber & Faber, 1945).

Greer, Rev. James, *The Windings of the Moy with Skreen and Tireragh*, (Dublin: Alex Thom, 1924).

Griffith, Sir Richard, *Primary Valuation of Ireland*, (Co. Mayo 1856-7).

Heffernan Farel, Thomas, *Wood Quay*, (Austin Univ. Texas Press, 1988).

Horgan, John, *Labour: The Price of Power*, (Dublin: Gill & Macmillan, 1986).

Lindsay, Patrick, *Memories*, (Dublin: Blackwater Press, 1993).

McGuire, James, *Steeple & People: The Story of Ballina & its Cathedral*, (Ballina: Western People, 1991).

Nealon, Ted, *Nealon's Guide to Dáil and Seanad Elections, 1973 to 1987*, (Dublin: Platform Press).

O'Brien, Conor Cruise, *States of Ireland*, (London: Hutchinson, 1972).

O'Reilly, Emily, *Candidate*, (Dublin: Attic Press, 1991).

Penniman, Howard R., *Ireland at the Polls: The Dáil Elections of 1977*, (Washington: American Enterprise Institute for Public Policy Research, 1978).

Ryan, Tim, *Mara, P.J.*, (Dublin: Blackwater Press, 1992).

Ryan, Tim, *A Safe Pair of Hands! The Unauthorised Biography of Dick Spring*, (Dublin: Blackwater Press, 1993).

Simington, Robert C., *The Transplantation to Connacht*, (Shannon: Irish University Press, 1970).

Smith, Raymond, *Garret the Enigma*, (Aherlow, 1985).

Smyth, John McG., *Theory and Practice of the Irish Senate*, (Dublin: Institute of Public Administration, 1972).

Spurling, Maj. Gen. J.M.K., *The Tigers: A Short History of the Royal Leicestershire Regiment*, (Leicestershire: Leicestershire Art Galleries & Records Services, 1982).

Whyte, John H., *Church and State in Modern Ireland 1923-1979*, (Dublin, Gill & Macmillan 1980).

APPENDIX I

Inauguration speech given by Her Excellency Mary Robinson, President of Ireland, in Dublin Castle on Monday 3 December 1990:

Citizens of Ireland, mná na hÉireann agus fir na hÉireann, you have chosen me to represent you and I am humbled by and grateful for your trust.

The Ireland I will be representing is a new Ireland, open, tolerant, inclusive. Many of you who voted for me did so without sharing all my views. This, I believe, is a significant signal of change, a sign, however modest, that we have already passed the threshold to a new, pluralist Ireland.

The recent revival of an old concept of the Fifth Province expresses this emerging Ireland of tolerance and empathy. The old Irish term for province is coicead, meaning "fifth" ; and yet, as everyone knows, there are only four geographical provinces on this island. So where is the fifth? The Fifth Province is not anywhere here or there, north or south, east or west. It is a place within each one of us - that place that is open to the other, that swinging door which allows us to venture out and others to venture in. Ancient legends divide Ireland into four quarters and a "middle", although they differed about the location of this middle or Fifth Province. While Tara was the political centre of Ireland, tradition has it that this Fifth Province acted as a second centre, a necessary balance. If I am a symbol of anything I would like to be a symbol of this reconciling and healing Fifth Province.

My primary role as President will be to represent this State. But the State is not the only model of community with which Irish people can and do identify. Beyond our State there is a vast community of Irish emigrants extending not only across our neighbouring island - which has provided a home away from home for several Irish generations - but also throughout the continents of North America, Australia and of course Europe itself. There are over 70 million people living on this globe who claim Irish descent. I will be proud to represent them. And I would like to see Áras an Uachtaráin, my official residence, serve - on something of an annual basis

- as a place where our emigrant communities could send representatives for a get-together of the extended Irish family abroad.

There is another level of community which I will represent. Not just the national, not just the global, but the local community. Within our State there are a growing number of local and regional communities determined to express their own creativity, identity, heritage and initiative in new and exciting ways. In my travels around Ireland I have found local community groups thriving on a new sense of self-confidence and self-empowerment. Whether it was groups concerned with adult education, employment initiative, women's support, local history and heritage, environmental concern or community culture, one of the most enriching discoveries was to witness the extent of this local empowerment at work.

As President I will seek to the best of my abilities to promote this growing sense of local participatory democracy, this emerging movement of self development and self expression which is surfacing more and more at grassroots level. This is the face of modern Ireland.

Ba mhaith liom a rá go bhfuair mé taithneamh agus pléisiúr as an taisteal a rinne mé le míosa anuas ar fuaid na hÉireann. Is fíor álainn agus iontach an tír atá againn, agus is álainn an pobal iad muintir na hÉireann.

Fuair mé teachtaireacht ón bpobal seo agus mé a dul timpeall: "Teastaíonn Uachtarán uainn gur féidir linn bheith bródúil aisti, ach, níos mó ná sin, gur féidir linn bheith bródúil lena chéile - toisc gur Éireannaigh sinn, agus go bhfuil traidisiúin agus cultúr álainn againn."

Is cuid an-tábhachtach don gcultúr sin an Ghaeilge - an teanga bheo - fé mar atá á labhairt sa Ghaeltacht agus ag daoine eile ar fuaid na hÉireann.

Tá aistear eile le déanamh anois agam - aistear cultúrtha, leis an saibhreas iontach atá sa teanga Ghaeilge a bhaint amach díom féin.

Tá súil agam go leanfaidh daoine eile mé atá ar mo nós féin - beagán as cleachtadh sa Ghaeilge - agus go raghaimíd ar aghaidh le chéile le taithneamh agus pléisiúr a fháil as ár dteanga álainn féin.

The best way we can contribute to a new and integrated Europe of the 1990s is by having a confident sense of our Irishness. Here again we must play to our strengths - take full advantage of our vibrant cultural

214

resources in music, art, drama, literature and film; value the role of our educators promote and preserve our unique enviornmental and geographical resources of relatively polution-free lakes, rivers, landscapes and seas; encourage and publicly support local initiative projects in aquaculture, forestry, fishing, alternative energy and smallscale technology.

Looking outwards from Ireland, I would like on your behalf to contribute to the international protection and promotion of human rights. One of our greatest natural resources has always been, and still is, our ability to serve as a moral and political conscience in world affairs. We have a long history in providing spiritual, cultural, and social assistance to other countries in need - most notably in Latin America, Africa and other Third World countries. And we can continue to promote these values by taking principled and independent stands on issues of international importance.

As the elected President of this small democratic country I assume office in a vital moment in Europe's history. Ideological boundaries that have separated East from West are withering away at an astounding pace. Eastern countries are seeking to participate as full partners in a restructured and economically buoyant Europe. The stage is set for a new common European home based on respect for human rights, pluralism, tolerance and openness to new ideas. The European Convention on human rights - one of the finest achievements of the Council of Europe - is asserting itself as the natural Constitution for the new Europe. These developments have created one of the major challenges for the 1990s.

If it is time, as Joyce's Stephen Dedalus remarked, that the Irish began to forge in the smithy of our souls "the uncreated conscience of our race" - might we not take on the still "uncreated conscience" of the wider international community? Is it not time that the small started believing again that it is beautiful, that the periphery can rise up and speak out on equal terms with the centre, that the most outlying island community of the European Community really has something "strange and precious" to contribute to the sea-change presently sweeping through the entire continent of Europe? As a native of Ballina, one of the most western towns of the most western province of the most western nation in

215

Europe, I want to say - "the West's awake".

I turn now to another place close to my heart, Northern Ireland. As the elected choice of the people of this part of our island I want to extend the hand of friendship and of love to both communities in the other part. And I want to do this with no hidden agendas, no strings attached. As the person chosen by you to symbolise this Republic and to project our self-image to others, I will seek to encourage mutual understanding and tolerance between all the different communities sharing this island.

In seeking to do this I shall rely to a large extent on symbols. But symbols are what unite and divide people. Symbols give us our identity, our self-image, our way of explaining ourselves to ourselves and to others. Symbols in turn determine the kinds of stories we tell; and the stories we tell determine the kind of history we make and remake. I want Áras an Uachtaráin to be a place where people can tell diverse stories - in the knowledge that there is someone there to listen.

I want this Presidency to promote the telling of stories - stories of celebration through the arts and stories of conscience and of social justice. As a woman, I want women who have felt themselves outside history to be written back into history, in the words of Eavan Boland, "finding a voice where they found a vision".

May God direct me so that my Presidency is one of justice, peace and love. May I have the fortune to preside over an Ireland at a time of exciting transformation when we enter a new Europe where old wounds can be healed, a time when, in the words of Seamus Heaney, "hope and history rhyme". May it be a Presidency where I, the President, can sing to you, citizens of Ireland, the joyous refrain of the 14th century Irish poet as recalled by W.B.Yeats:

"I am of Ireland... come dance with me in Ireland."

Go raibh míle maith agaibh go léir.

APPENDIX II

Select index, arranged alphabetically, of reported cases in which Mary Robinson appeared. The main citations are from the Irish Reports (IR) and from the Irish Law Reports Monthly (ILRM).

Abdelkefi v Minister for Justice [1984] ILRM 138.

Aer Lingus Teo. v The Labour Court [1990] ILRM 485.

Ahern v Kerry County Council [1988] ILRM 392.

Airey v Ireland, judgment 9 Oct 1979, Series A vol 32.

An Chómhairle Oiliúna Talamhaíochta v Doyle [1989] IR 33; [1990] ILRM 21.

Attorney General (Martin) v Dublin Corporation, High Court Unreported, 12th Feb 1979; Supreme Court, Unreported, 7th March 1979; [1983] ILRM 254; Application No. 8569/79 European Commission of Human Rights.

Attorney General (SPUC Ltd) v Open Door Counselling Ltd. [1988] IR 593; [1987] ILRM 477; [1989] ILRM 19.

Cadwell v The Labour Court [1988] IR 280.

Cafolla v Attorney General [1985] IR 486; [1986] ILRM 177

Cannon v Minister for the Marine [1991] 1 IR 82; [1991] ILRM 261.

Conlon v Mohamed [1987] ILRM 172; [1989] ILRM 523.

Containercare Ltd v Wycherley [1982] IR 143.

Cork Corporation v Cahill [1987] IR 478.

Cosgrave v Ireland [1982] ILRM 48.

de Burca v Attorney General [1976] IR 38.

Devitt v Minister for Education [1989] ILRM 639.

Director of Public Prosecutions v McLoughlin [1986] IR 355; [1986] ILRM 493.

Donohoe v Browne [1986] IR 90.

Doyle v An Taoiseach and Others [1981] ECR 735.

Dublin Well Woman Centre v Ireland, Application No. 14235/88 European Commission of Human Rights

Duggan v An Taoiseach [1989] ILRM 710.

E. v E. [1982] ILRM 497.

M.F. v The Superintendent, Ballymun Garda Station [1991] I IR 189; [1990] ILRM 243, 767.

Flynn v An Post [1987] IR 68.

Flynn v Director of Public Prosecutions [1986] ILRM 290.

Foley v Moulton [1989] ILRM 169.

Geraghty v Rohan Industrial Estates Ltd. [1988] IR 419.

Harvey v Minister for Social Welfare [1990] 2 IR 232; [1990] ILRM 185.

Healy v Eastern Health Board [1988] IR 747.

Hyland v Minister for Social Welfare [1989] IR 624; [1989] ILRM 196; [1990] ILRM 213.

Inspector of Taxes Assoc. v Minister for Public Service [1986] ILRM 296.

Irish Family Planning Assoc. v Ryan [1979] IR 295.

Ivory v Ski-Line Ltd [1988] IR 399; ILRM 433.

Johnston & Others v Ireland, Judgment 18 December 1986, Series A vol. 112.

K v An Bórd Altranais [1990] 2 IR 396.

K v W [1990] 2 IR 437; [1990] ILRM 121, 791.

Kennedy v Hearne [1987] IR 120; [1988] IR 481; [1988] ILRM 52, 531.

Kennedy v Ireland [1987] IR 587; [1988] ILRM 472.

Lee v Minister for Agriculture (1980) ECR 1495.

M v An Bórd Uchtala [1975] IR 81.

C.M. v T.M. [1987] IR 152; [1990] 2 IR 52; [1988] ILRM 262, 456; [1991] ILRM 268.

J.M. and G.M. v An Bórd Uchtala [1988] ILRM 203.

McDermott and Cotter v Minister for Social Welfare [1987] ILRM 324; [1987] 2 CMLR 607; (1987) ECR 1453.

McGrath and O'Ruairc v The Trustees of Maynooth College [1979] ILRM 166.

McHugh v Commissioner of An Garda Síochána [1986] IR 228; [1985] ILRM 606; [1987] ILRM 181.

MacMathuna v Attorney General [1989] IR 504.

Muckley v Ireland [1985] IR 472; [1986] ILRM 364.

Murphy v An Bórd Telecom Éireann [1986] ILRM 483; [1989] ILRM 53; [1988] I CMLR 879; (1988) ECR 673.

Murphy v Attorney General [1982] IR 241.

Murphy v Minister for Social Welfare [1987] IR 295.

Mythen v Employment Appeals Tribunal [1989] ILRM 844.

N (otherwise K v K) [1985] IR 733; [1986] ILRM 75.

Nolan v Minister for the Environment [1989] IR 357.

Norris v Attorney General and Ireland [1984] IR 36; Judgment 26 Oct 1988 Series A vol. 142.

North Western Health Board v Martyn [1988] ILRM 519.

O'B v O'B [1984] IR 182; [1984] ILRM 1.

O'Brien v Bórd na Móna [1983] IR 255; [1983] ILRM 314.

O'Brien v Stoutt [1984] IR 316; [1982] ILRM 327; [1985] ILRM 86; Application No. 10978 European Comm. of Human Rights.

O'Dowd v North Western Health Board [1983] ILRM 186.

O'Reilly v Limerick Corporation [1989] ILRM 181.

Osheku v Ireland [1986] IR 733; [1987] ILRM 330.

Pok Sun Shum v Ireland [1986] ILRM 593.

Quirke v Folio Homes Ltd [1988] ILRM 496.

R v R [1984] IR 296.

Reynolds v Attorney General, High Court Unreported 16 Feb. 1973.

SPUC v Grogan [1989] IR 753; [1990] ILRM 350; [1992] ILRM 461.

State (DPP) v Walsh [1981] IR 412.

State (Gallagher Shatter and Co.) v de Valera [1991] 2 IR 198.

State (Kenny) v Minister for Social Welfare [1986] IR 693.

State (M) v Attorney General [1979] IR 73.

State (Murphy) v Governor of St Patrick's Institution [1984] IR 458; [1982] ILRM 475; [1985] ILRM 141.

T v T [1983] IR 29.

Thompson v Minister for Social Welfare [1989] IR 618.

Webb v Ireland [1988] IR 353; [1988] ILRM 565.

Williams & Others v Ireland Application No. 9596/81 European Commission of Human Rights.

INDEX